classic knits

MARIANNE ISAGER COLLECTION

INTERWEAVE
interweavestore.com

EDITOR Ann Budd
TECHNICAL EDITOR Kristen TenDyke
TRANSLATION Carol H. Rhoades
COVER & INTERIOR DESIGN Pamela Norman
PAGE LAYOUT Jillfrances Gray
MODEL & SWATCH PHOTOGRAPHY Tove Petersen
ILLUSTRATION Åse Lund Jensen
TECHNICAL ILLUSTRATION Gayle Ford
PROJECT DETAIL PHOTOGRAPHY Joe Coca and Annette Slade
PRODUCTION Katherine Jackson

Text © 2009 Marianne Isager
Project detail photography © 2009 Interweave Press LLC

Interweave Press LLC
201 East Fourth Street
Loveland, CO 80537-5655 USA
interweavestore.com

Printed in China by Asia Pacific Offset.

Library of Congress Cataloging-in-Publication Data

Isager, Marianne, 1954-
  Classic knits : Marianne Isager collection / Marianne Isager, author.
     p. cwm.
  Includes index.
  ISBN 978-1-59668-115-6
  1. Knitting--Patterns. 2. Knitwear. I. Title.
  TT825.I825 2009
  746.43'2041--dc22
                              2008038787

10 9 8 7 6 5 4 3 2 1

acknowledgments

Thank you to Åse Lund Jensen for leaving me her work drawings, many of which I have used in this book. Her work has also provided me with constant inspiration.

Thank you to my diligent knitters and co-workers—without your help and support, this book would never have been possible!

table of contents

ORIGINALLY PUBLISHED in Danish as *Strik a la Carte, Classic Knits* is a collection of handknitted garments as well as an instruction book. You can choose the techniques you'd like to learn and apply them to your own designs.

Although the garments have classic styling with many fine details, they are quite easy to knit. Each pattern starts with a gauge swatch that includes all the techniques that will be used in the garment. If your swatch is knitted to the correct gauge, then your garment will end up with the measurements listed in the pattern. Feel free to experiment and substitute other yarns as long they knit up to the same gauge.

The yarns I recommend are high-quality wool, linen, and cotton. It takes a lot of time to produce a handknitted garment, and this merits a yarn that looks nice and wears well over time. Also, you'll find that the knitting is much more enjoyable when quality materials are used that will ensure a beautiful finished garment.

Many of the garments in this book are based on simple knit-purl pattern stitches. None require extensive knitting experience. You only need to know how to cast on, knit, and bind off to successfully complete any project in this book. All the other information is provided in sidebars and the Glossary.

Many knitters have trouble with the finishing process. For that reason, I've designed garments that need as little finishing as possible. I've also designed several garments to be worked from the top down so that it's easy to add or remove rows to adjust the length to your preference.

The models in the book are drawn from my best designs, with a little extra "spice" added. I hope that they will give you pleasure and enjoyment both in knitting and wearing.

With very best wishes from

Marianne

corsage

This garter-stitch top is decorated with narrow relief ribs that add a slimming, feminine fit. The top is worked from the shoulders down to the hem, making it easy to adjust for the desired total length. The stitches of the relief ribs are slipped on all wrong-side rows and all other stitches are knitted every row. Knitted in a combination of cotton and linen yarns, this top is comfortable and durable.

FINISHED SIZE
About 28¼ (31¼, 34¾)" (72 [79.5, 88.5] cm) bust circumference, buttoned. Sweater shown measures 31¼" (79.5 cm).

YARN
About 100 (150, 200) grams of a main color (MC1) of fingering-weight (#1 Super Fine) yarn and about 100 (150, 200) grams of a main color (MC2) of another fingering-weight yarn, used held together.

Shown here: **Viscolin** (50% viscose, 50% linen; 202 yd [185 m]/50 g): #43 olive (MC1), 2 (3, 4) skeins. **Bomuld** (100% cotton; 459 yd [420 m]/50 g): #43 olive (MC2), 2 (3, 4) skeins.

NEEDLES
Size U.S. 4 (3.5 mm): straight and 24" (60 cm) circular (cir). Adjust needle size if necessary to obtain the correct gauge.

NOTIONS
Tapestry needle; stitch holders; twelve ⁵⁄₈" (1.5 cm) buttons.

GAUGE
22 stitches and 39 rows = 4" (10 cm) in garter stitch with one strand each of MC1 and MC2 held together, slightly stretched vertically.

NOTES
+ Work with one strand of each of MC1 and MC2 held together throughout.

+ The top is knitted from the top down, beginning with the back strap.

+ Slip stitches purlwise with yarn in front (pwise wyf) on wrong-side rows.

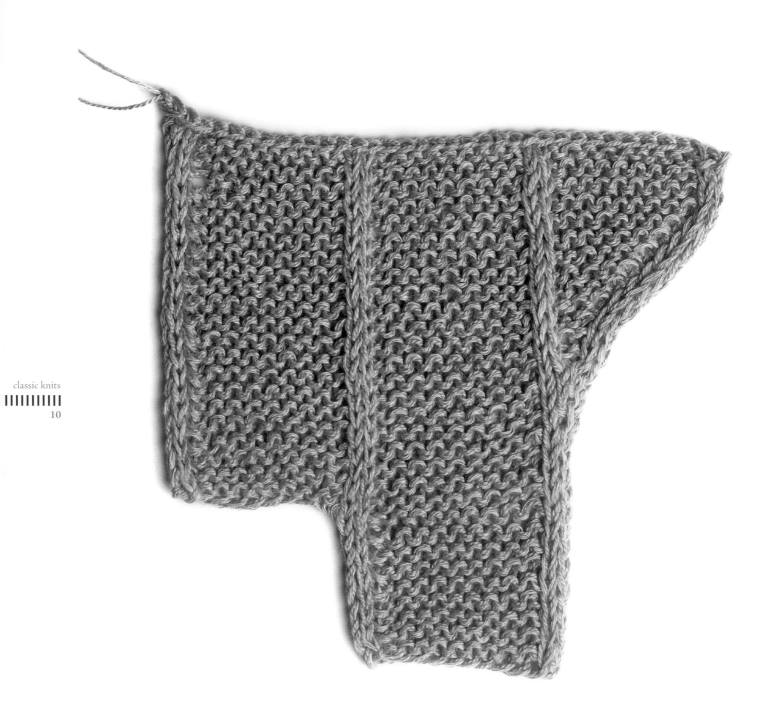

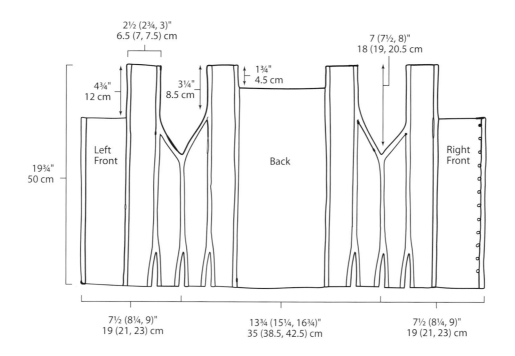

2½ (2¾, 3)"
6.5 (7, 7.5) cm

7 (7½, 8)"
18 (19, 20.5 cm

4¾"
12 cm

3¼"
8.5 cm

1¾"
4.5 cm

Left
Front

Back

Right
Front

19¾"
50 cm

7½ (8¼, 9)"
19 (21, 23) cm

13¾ (15¼, 16¾)"
35 (38.5, 42.5) cm

7½ (8¼, 9)"
19 (21, 23) cm

GAUGE SWATCH

With one strand of each yarn held tog and using the long-tail method (see Glossary), CO 15 sts.

ROW 1: (WS) Sl 1 pwise wyf (edge st), sl 2 (see Notes), k9, sl 2, k1 (edge st).

ROW 2: (RS) Sl 1 pwise wyf (edge st), knit to end.

Rep Rows 1 and 2 eight more times, ending with a RS row—9 garter ridges. Using the knitted method (see Glossary), CO 11 more sts—26 sts total.

ROW 3: (WS) Sl 1 pwise wyf, [sl 2, k9] 2 times, sl 2, k1.

ROW 4: (RS) Sl 1 wyf, knit to end.

Rep Rows 3 and 4 three more times, then rep Row 3 once more—14 garter ridges total.

Work 10-row armhole set-up as foll.

ROW 1: (RS) Sl 1 pwise wyf, k1, M1 (see Glossary), knit to end—27 sts.

ROW 2: (WS) Work as established to last 4 sts, sl 3, k1.

ROW 3: Sl 1 pwise wyf, k2, M1, knit to end—28 sts.

ROWS 4 AND 6: Work as established to last 5 sts, sl 4, k1.

ROWS 5 AND 9: Sl 1 pwise wyf, knit to end.

ROW 7: Rep Row 3—29 sts.

ROW 8: Work as established to last 6 sts, [sl 2, k1] 2 times.

ROW 10: Rep Row 8—19 garter ridges total.

INC ROW: (RS) Sl 1 pwise wyf, k2, M1, knit to end— 1 st inc'd.

Work 1 WS row even. Rep the last 2 rows 8 more times, working inc'd sts in garter st—38 sts. Work even for 3 rows, ending with a WS row. With RS facing, BO all sts knitwise (kwise).

Block as described on page 33.

TOP
Back Straps

With one strand of each yarn held tog, straight needles, and using the long-tail method (see Glossary), CO 14 (15, 16) sts.

ROW 1: (WS) Sl 1 pwise wyf (edge st), sl 2 (see Notes), k8 (9, 10), sl 2, k1 (edge st).
ROW 2: (RS) Sl 1 pwise wyf, knit to end.

Rep Rows 1 and 2 seven more times, then work Row 1 once more—9 garter ridges. Cut yarn and place sts on holder. Make another piece to match, but do not cut yarn and leave sts on needle.

BACK

JOINING ROW: With RS facing and keeping in patt as established, work 14 (15, 16) sts of strap, use the backward-loop method (see Glossary) to CO 32 (36, 40) sts, work 14 (15, 16) sts of other strap—60 (66, 72) sts total.
ROW 1: (WS) Sl 3, k8 (9, 10), sl 2, knit to last 13 (14, 15) sts, sl 2, k8 (9, 10), sl 2, k1.
ROW 2: (RS) Sl 1 pwise wyf, knit to end.

Rep these 2 rows 6 more times, then work Row 1 once more—7 garter ridges from joining row; piece measures 1½" (3.8 cm) from joining row.

Shape Armholes

Work 10 armhole set-up rows as foll.

ROW 1: (RS) Sl 1 pwise wyf, k1, M1 (see Glossary), knit to last st, M1, k1—62 (68, 74) sts.
ROW 2: (WS) Sl 4, work in established patt to last 4 sts, sl 3, k1.
ROW 3: Sl 1 pwise wyf, k2, M1, knit to last 3 sts, M1, k3—64 (70, 76) sts.
ROWS 4 AND 6: Sl 4, work in established patt to last 5 sts, sl 4, k1.
ROWS 5 AND 9: Sl 1 pwise wyf, knit to end.
ROW 7: Rep Row 3—66 (72, 78) sts.

ROW 8: Sl 1 pwise wyf, [sl 2, k1] 2 times, work in established patt to last 6 sts, [sl 2, k1] 2 times.

ROW 10: Rep Row 8—12 garter ridges from joining row.

Cont in patt, inc as foll.

INC ROW: (RS) Sl 1 pwise wyf, k2, M1, work in established patt to last 3 sts, M1, k3—2 sts inc'd.

Work 3 rows even in patt. Rep the last 4 rows 6 (7, 8) more times, ending with a WS row—80 (88, 96) sts; 8 (9, 10) sts between relief sts at each side. Place sts on holder.

RIGHT FRONT

With RS facing, pick up and knit 14 (15, 16) sts along the CO edge of right back strap. Work as for the back strap until a total of 22 garter ridges have been worked, ending with a RS row—piece measures about 4½" (11.5 cm) from pick-up row.

JOINING ROW: (RS) Use the backward-loop method to CO 19 (21, 23) sts for center front—33 (36, 39) sts total.

ROW 1: (WS) Sl 3, knit to last 13 (14, 15) sts, sl 2, k8 (9, 10), sl 2, k1.

ROW 2: (RS) Sl 1 pwsie wyf, knit to end.

Rep Row 1 once more.

BUTTONHOLE ROW: (RS) Sl 1 pwise wyf, knit to last 5 sts, k2tog, k3.

NEXT ROW: (WS) Sl 3, use the backward-loop method to CO 1 st over the k2tog of previous row to complete buttonhole, work to end as for Row 1.

Keeping in patt, rep buttonhole row every 10th row (after every 5th garter ridge) 11 more times. *At the same time* when piece measures 5 (5¼, 5½)" (12.5 [13.5, 14] cm) from pick-up row, ending with a WS row, shape armhole.

Shape Armhole

Cont in patt, working buttonholes as specified and *at the same time* work 10 armhole set-up rows as foll.

ROW 1: (RS) Sl 1 pwise wyf, k1, M1, knit to end—34 (37, 40) sts.

ROW 2: (WS) Sl 3, work in established patt to last 4 sts, sl 3, k1.

ROW 3: Sl 1 pwise wyf, k2, M1, knit to end—35 (38, 41) sts.

ROWS 4 AND 6: Sl 3, work in established patt to last 5 sts, sl 4, k1.

ROWS 5 AND 9: Sl 1 pwise wyf, knit to end.

ROW 7: Rep Row 3—36 (39, 42) sts.

ROW 8: Sl 3, work in established patt to last 6 sts, [sl 2, k1] 2 times.

ROW 10: Rep Row 8.

Cont in patt, inc at armhole edge as foll.

INC ROW: (RS) Sl 1 pwise wyf, k2, M1, knit to end—1 st inc'd.

Work 1 WS row even. Rep the last 2 rows 6 (7, 8) times, ending with a WS row—43 (47, 51) sts; 8 (9, 10) sts between relief sts at side. Place sts on holder.

Back

LEFT FRONT

With RS facing, pick up and knit 14 (15, 16) sts along the CO edge of left back strap. Work as for the back strap until a total of 22 garter ridges have been worked, ending with a WS row—piece measures 4½" (11.5) from pick-up row. With WS still facing, use the backward-loop method to CO 19 (21, 23) sts for center front—33 (36, 39) sts total.

ROW 1: (RS) Sl 1 pwise wyf, knit to end.

ROW 2: (WS) Sl 3, k8 (9, 10), sl 2, work in established patt to last 3 sts, sl 2, k1.

Rep Rows 1 and 2 until piece measures 5 (5¼, 5½)" (12.5 [13.5, 14] cm) from pick-up row, ending with a WS row.

Shape Armhole

Work 10 armhole set-up rows as foll.

ROW 1: (RS) Sl 1 pwise wyf, knit to last st, M1, k1—34 (37, 40) sts.

ROW 2: (WS) Sl 4, work in established patt to last 3 sts, sl 2, k1.

ROW 3: Sl 1 pwise wyf, knit to last 3 sts, M1, k3—35 (38, 41) sts.

ROWS 4 AND 6: Sl 4, work in established patt to last 3 sts, sl 2, k1.

ROWS 5 AND 9: Sl 1 pwise wyf, knit to end.

ROW 7: Rep Row 3—36 (39, 42) sts.

ROW 8: Sl 1 pwise wyf, [sl 2, k1] 2 times, work in established patt to last 3 sts, sl 2, k1.

ROW 10: Rep Row 8.

Cont in patt, inc at armhole edge as foll.

INC ROW: (RS) Sl 3, work in established patt to last 3 sts, M1, k3—1 st inc'd.

Work 1 WS row even. Rep the last 2 rows 6 (7, 8) times, ending with a WS row—43 (47, 51) sts; 8 (9, 10) sts between relief sts at side.

JOIN FRONTS AND BACK

With RS facing, place sts on cir needle as foll: 43 (47, 51) left front sts, place marker (pm), 80 (88, 96) back sts, pm, 43 (47, 51) right front sts—166 (182, 198) sts total.

DEC ROW: (RS) Keeping in patt, sl 1 pwise wyf, *work to 3 sts before m, k3tog, slip m (sl m), k3tog; rep from * once, work to end—158 (174, 190) sts rem; 2 relief rib sts at each side at underarm.

Knitting these 2 relief sts on RS rows and slipping them pwise wyf on WS rows, work even as established until piece measures 2" (5 cm) from joining row, ending with a WS row.

DEC ROW: (RS) *Work in patt to 3 sts before side seam m, k2tog, k1, sl m, k1, ssk; rep from * once, work to end—4 sts dec'd.

Work 19 rows even. Rep the last 20 rows 3 more times—142 (158, 174) sts rem. Work even as established until piece measures 10" (25.5 cm) from joining row, or 5" (12.5 cm) less than desired length, working a total of 12 buttonholes and ending with a WS row.

Hem Slits

Mark each relief rib before and after each side seam relief rib on fronts and back, placing the marker between the two relief sts. Remove side seam markers. Work 10-row set-up, working incs within marked relief ribs, as foll.

ROW 1: (RS) Sl 1 pwise wyf, *knit to m, sl m, M1; rep from * 3 times, knit to end—4 sts inc'd.

ROW 2: (WS) Sl 3, *work in patt to 2 sts before m, sl 2, sl m, sl 1; rep from * 3 times, work to end in patt.

ROW 3: Rep Row 1—4 sts inc'd.

ROW 4: Sl 3, *work in patt to 3 sts before m, sl 3, sl m, sl 1; rep from * 3 times, work to end in patt.

ROW 5: Sl 1 pwise wyb, *knit to m, sl m, k1, M1; rep from * 3 times, knit to end—4 sts inc'd.

ROW 6: Sl 3, *work in patt to 4 sts before m, sl 2, k1, sl 2, sl m; rep from * 3 times, work to end in patt.

ROW 7: Sl 1 pwise wyb, *knit to m, sl m, k2, M1; rep from * 3 times, knit to end—4 sts inc'd; 158 (174, 190) sts.

ROW 8: Sl 3, *work in patt to 5 sts before m, sl 2, k2, sl 1, sl m, sl 1; rep from * 3 times, work to end in patt.

ROW 9: Sl 1 pwise wyb, knit to end.

ROW 10: Rep Row 8.

Make Slits in Marked Relief Ribs

With RS facing, *work to m, remove m, k2, turn, leaving rem sts unworked. Cont as established, work this section separately until slit measures about 4" (10 cm) from top of shoulder, or desired length, ending with a WS row. With RS facing, BO all sts for this section kwise. Cut yarn. Rejoin yarn to next section with RS and BO all sts kwise.

FINISHING

Lay garment flat under a damp cloth to block. Weave in loose ends. Sew buttons to left front, opposite buttonholes.

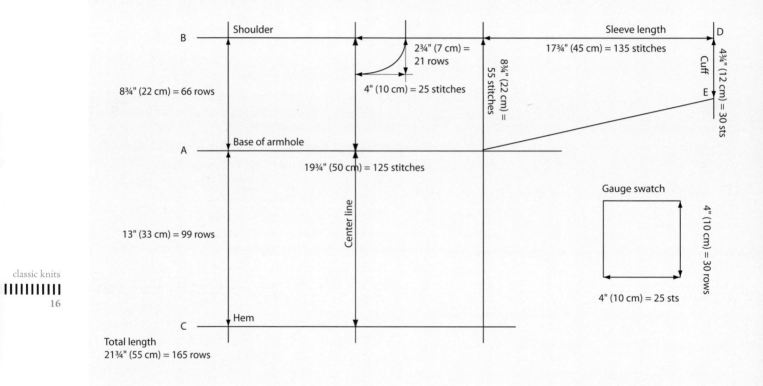

B Shoulder

2¾" (7 cm) = 21 rows

4" (10 cm) = 25 stitches

Sleeve length

17¾" (45 cm) = 135 stitches

D

8¾" (22 cm) = 55 stitches

4¾" (12 cm) = 30 sts

Cuff

8¾" (22 cm) = 66 rows

E

A Base of armhole

19¾" (50 cm) = 125 stitches

Center line

13" (33 cm) = 99 rows

Gauge swatch

4" (10 cm) = 30 rows

4" (10 cm) = 25 sts

Hem

C

Total length
21¾" (55 cm) = 165 rows

technique: adjusting sizes

|||||||||||||||||||||||||||||||||||||||||||||||||||||||||||||||||||||||||||||||||||||||||||||||||||||||

Calculating Sizes

With a little practice, you can learn how to calculate the sizing for your own designs. You'll need some plain white paper, pencil, red pencil, drafting triangle, ruler, and an eraser. To begin, use the red pencil to draw a vertical line on the paper to represent the centerline of a sweater. Use the drafting triangle to help you draw a horizontal line across the vertical line to represent the base of the armholes. All measurements will be based on these two lines.

Create a Schematic

To create a simple schematic, measure a sweater that fits you well and transfer these measurements onto the paper, using the red lines as guidelines. Measure the chest width (half of the chest circumference; A) on the horizontal line, and draw two vertical lines centered over the centerline to indicate the body width. Measure the armhole depth (B) up from the horizontal line and draw another horizontal to indicate the top of the shoulders. Measure the total body length (from shoulder to hem) down from the shoulder line and draw another horizontal line to indicate the hem (C). Measure the distance from the center back neck to the end of the sleeve cuff along the shoulder line and draw a vertical line to indicate the cuff edge of the sleeve (D). Measure the cuff width (half of the cuff circumference) down from the shoulder line and mark this as Point E on the cuff line. Draw a tapered line from Point E to the horizontal line at the base of the armhole to indicate the width (half the circumference) of the upper sleeve at the armhole. Finally, measure the width and depth of the neck opening and add these measurements. For the example shown, the body width is 19¾" (50 cm), the length to the armhole is 13" (33 cm), the armhole length is 8¾" (22 cm), the sleeve length is 17¾" (45 cm), and the cuff width is 4¾" (12 cm). The neck is 8" (20.5 cm) wide and 2¾" (7 cm) deep.

This is a very simple outline, but as you can imagine, the more detail you add to the schematic in terms of shaping the shoulders, armholes, and waist, for example, the more refined the garment will be.

Determine Body Stitch and Row Counts

To convert these measurements to number of stitches and rows, write down the stitch gauge and row gauge per inch of knitting, including partial stitches or rows. For example, if your gauge is 25 stitches and 30 rows per 4" (10 cm), there will be 6.25 stitches and 7.5 rows per inch (2.5 cm). To calculate stitches, multiply the width measurements by the stitch gauge. For example, the body width of 19¾" (50 cm) would require $19.75 \times 6.25 = 123.4$ stitches. You need to work in full numbers of stitches so you'd round this number up to 124 stitches or down to 123 stitches, depending if the pattern stitch you've chosen requires an even or odd number of stitches. To calculate rows, multiply the length measurement by the row gauge. For example, the number of rows to work the body 13" (33 cm) to the armhole would be $13 \times 7.5 = 97.5$ rows. Again, you'll want to round this up to an even 98 rows or down to and odd 97 rows.

DETERMINE SLEEVE STITCH AND ROW COUNTS

The sleeve drawn on the schematic is only the front half of the actual sleeve. Multiplying these widths at the cuff and upper sleeve will only give half the total number of stitches required. For example, the 8¾" (22 cm) measurement at the top of sleeve translates to 55 stitches ($8.75 \times 6.25 = 54.6$ stitches, which we'll round up to 55), and the 4¾" (12 cm) measurement at the cuff translates to 30 stitches ($4.75 \times 6.25 = 29.7$ stitches, which we'll round up to 30). But these numbers account for only the front half of the sleeve. Therefore each needs to be multiplied by 2 to get the total circumferences—110 stitches at the top and 60 stitches at the cuff.

Notice how the sleeve tapers from the cuff to the armhole. In terms of stitches, there's a difference of $110 - 60 = 50$ stitches between the cuff and the armhole. Depending on whether you plan to work the sleeve from the top down or from the bottom up, you will have to decrease or increase these stitches evenly spaced along the way. According to the schematic, the 17¾" (45 cm) sleeve length requires $17.75 \times 7.5 = 133.1$ rows, which we'll round down to 132. To make a symmetrical shape, the 50 decreases should be split between the two sides of the sleeve—each side of a center stitch at the underarm. Therefore, we know that of the 132 total sleeve rows, 25 of them will be decrease or increase rows (2 stitches decreased or increased in each shaping row). To calculate how to space the shaping rows, divide the total number of rows by the number of shaping rows: $132 \div 25 = 5.28$. This means you'll work the decreases or increases every 5th row, with a few rows of plain knitting at the end. Because it is usually easiest to work decreases or increases on right-side rows, you may want to work the shaping alternately every 4th and 6th row.

DETERMINE NECK OPENING STITCH AND ROW COUNTS

All that's left is to calculate the neck opening. If the opening will be symmetrical, we only need to calculate half of it—the other half will be a mirror image. According to the schematic example, half of the neck width is 4" (10 cm). In stitches, this translates to $4 \times 6.25 = 25$ stitches. The neck drops 2¾" (7 cm) from the shoulder line, which translates to $2.75 \times 7.5 = 20.6$ rows, which we'll round up to 21 rows. To produce this shape, 25 stitches will have to be eliminated over 21 rows. For a nice, rounded shape, we'll want to begin with several stitches bound off, then taper to fewer and fewer stitches each shaping row. Because we can only bind off at the beginning of rows, we have to accomplish this shaping over 10 rows (the other rows are "return" rows that will have no shaping). I generally like to devise a sequence to space out the decreases evenly, but you could just as well mark the rows and stitches on graph paper and draw a neckline that matches. For example, bind off the center 8 stitches on the first neck row, then at subsequent rows that begin at the neck edge, bind off 4 stitches once, then bind off 3 stitches 2 times, then bind off 2 stitches 2 times, then bind off 1 stitch 3 times.

The more patterns you work out on paper, the easier it will become. Armed with such a schematic and calculations, you'll be able to knit an entire sweater without any instructions other than the pattern stitch. If the pattern has a particular repeat—a set number of stitches and rows that are repeated for the pattern—you'll need to take that into consideration when calculating the stitch and row counts. And you'll want to be sure to add an edge stitch at each selvedge for seaming.

cossack

FINISHED SIZE
About 34¼ (38¼, 41)" (87 [97, 104] cm)
bust circumference, buttoned. Sweater shown measures 38¼" (97 cm).

YARN
About 150 (200, 250) grams of a main color (MC1) and 100 grams of a contrasting color (CC) of fingering weight (#1 Super Fine) yarn. About 100 (150, 200) grams of a main color (MC2) of laceweight (#0 Lace) yarn.

Shown here: **Highland** (100% wool; 305 yd [279 m]/50 g): Oxford (MC1), 3 (4, 5) skeins. **Alpaca 2** (50% merino, 50% alpaca; 270 yd [247 m]/50 g): #016 chartreuse (CC), 1 (1, 1) skein. **Alpaca 1** (100% alpaca; 437 yd [400 m]/50 g): #500 black (MC2), 2 (3, 4) skeins.

NEEDLES
Size U.S. 2 (3.0 mm): 34" and 16" (80 and 16 cm) circular (cir) and set of 4 or 5 double-pointed (dpn). Adjust needle size if necessary to obtain the correct gauge.

NOTIONS
Markers (m); stitch holders; tapestry needle; nine ⁵⁄₈" (1.5 cm) buttons; fur or fake-fur collar (optional).

GAUGE
23 stitches and 30 rows = 4" (10 cm) in k2, p2 ribbing with one strand each of MC1 and MC2 held together, slightly stretched.

As for Corsage and many other garments in this book, Cossack is worked from the top down. Once the raglan shaping is established, the sweater is easy to knit in knit-two-purl-two ribbing. The peplum at the lower edge is worked with an extra strand of yarn and more stitches in knit-two-purl-three ribbing. The elasticity of the rib pattern gives the body a fitted look.

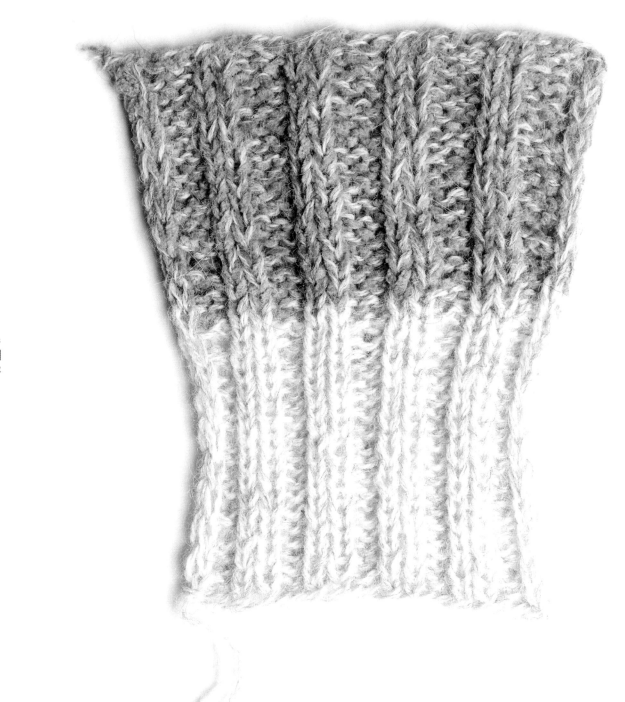

GAUGE SWATCH

With one strand each of MC1 and MC2 held tog and using the long-tail method (see Glossary), CO 22 sts.

ROW 1: (WS) Sl 2 (see Notes), *k2, p2; rep from * to last 4 sts, k2, p1, k1.

ROW 2: Sl 1 pwise with yarn in front (wyf), sl 1 pwise with yarn in back (wyb), *p2, k2; rep from *.

Rep Rows 1 and 2 until piece measures 2¾" (7 cm) from CO, ending with a RS row.

INC ROW: (WS) Sl 2, *k1, M1 (see Glossary), k1, p2; rep from * to last 4 sts, k1, M1, k1—27 sts.

Join CC. Working with all three strands held tog and working 2 sts at each edge as established, work center sts in k2, p3 rib as established for 2½" (6.5 cm), ending with a WS row. With RS facing, BO all sts in patt.

Block as described on page 33.

YOKE

With long cir needle and one strand each of MC1 and MC2 held tog, CO 52 sts. Work back and forth in rows as foll: (WS) K1, p2, place markers (pm) each side of the previous 2 purl sts for right front marked sts, [k2, p2] 2 times, pm each side of previous 2 purl sts for right back marked sts, [k2, p2] 8 times, pm each side of previous 2 purl sts for left back marked sts, [k2, p2] 2 times, pm each side of previous 2 purl sts for left front marked sts, k1. Slip markers every row.

ROW 1: (RS) Keeping in rib patt as established, *work to marker, M1 (see Glossary), sl m, k2, sl m, M1; rep from * 3 more times, work to end—8 sts inc'd; 60 sts total.

ROW 2: (WS) Work in rib as established, working the marked sts in St st (knit RS rows; purl WS rows) and the inc'd sts in rib patt as they become available.

INC ROW: (RS) K1 (edge st; work in St st), M1, *keeping sts in rib as established, work to marker, M1, sl m, k2,

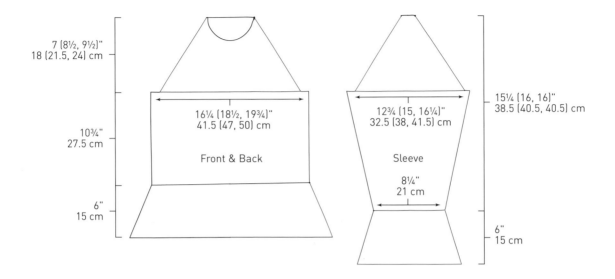

Front & Back

7 (8½, 9½)"
18 (21.5, 24) cm

16¼ (18½, 19¾)"
41.5 (47, 50) cm

10¾"
27.5 cm

6"
15 cm

Sleeve

12¾ (15, 16¼)"
32.5 (38, 41.5) cm

15¼ (16, 16)"
38.5 (40.5, 40.5) cm

8¼"
21 cm

6"
15 cm

sl m, M1; rep from * 3 more times, work to last st, M1, k1 (edge st; work in St st)—10 sts inc'd.

Work 1 WS row even. Rep the last 2 rows 8 more times—150 sts; 20 sts outside marked sts each front; 26 sts outside marked sts each sleeve; 50 sts outside marked sts for back. Rep Rows 1 and 2 and *at the same time* use the backward-loop method (see Glossary) to CO at each neck edge as foll: CO 2 sts 2 times, then CO 4 sts 1 time, working inc'd sts in k2, p2 rib and ending after a RS row—190 sts; 31 sts outside marked sts each front; 32 sts outside marked sts each sleeve; 56 sts outside marked sts for back. Work Rows 1 and 2 once more and *at the same time* CO 4 sts at beg of each row; keep these 4 sts in St st—206 sts; 36 sts each front; 34 sts each sleeve; 58 sts for back.

NEXT ROW: (RS) Sl 1 pwise wyf, sl 1 pwise wyb, k2, *work in rib as established to m, M1, sl m, k2, sl m, M1; rep from * 3 more times, work in rib as est to last 4 sts, k4—8 sts inc'd.
NEXT ROW: (WS) Sl 2, work in rib as established to last 4 sts, p4.

Rep the last 2 rows 11 (17, 21) more times and *at the same time* when piece measures ¾" (2 cm) from last st of CO sts, work buttonhole as foll.

BUTTONHOLE ROW: (RS) Work to last 6 sts, yo, p2tog, k4.

Rep buttonhole row every 1½" (3.8 cm) until there are 9 buttonholes total. When yoke shaping is complete there will be 302 (350, 382) sts; 48 (54, 58) sts outside marked sts each front; 58 (70, 78) sts outside marked sts each sleeve; 82 (94, 102) sts outside marked sts for back. Work 1 WS row even.

DIVIDE FOR FRONTS, BACK, AND SLEEVES
(RS) Work to m, remove m, using the backward-loop method, CO 12 sts for underarm, sl next 62 (74, 82) unworked sts to holder for sleeve (remove markers as you go), work 82 (94, 102) back sts to next m, remove m, CO 12 sts as before, sl next 62 (74, 82) unworked sts to holder for sleeve (remove markers as you go), work to end—202 (226, 242) sts rem.

LOWER BODY

Cont working buttonholes every 1½" (3.8 cm) as established, work even until piece measures 10¾" (27.5 cm) from armhole, ending with a RS row—9 buttonholes total.

INC ROW: (WS) Sl 2, p2, *k1, M1, k1, p2; rep from * to last 2 sts, p2—251 (281, 301) sts.

Peplum

Join CC. With one strand each of MC1, MC2, and CC held tog, work in k2, p3 rib until piece measures 6" (15 cm) from color change, slipping the first 2 sts of every row as established to keep edge sts firm. BO all sts in patt.

Sleeves

Place 62 (74, 82) held sleeve sts on short cir needle. With one strand each of MC1 and MC2 held tog and RS facing, pick up and knit 12 sts along CO edge of underarm—74 (86, 94) sts. Join for working in rnds and pm between 2 center sts of 12 underarm sts. Work in k2, p2 rib as established for 7 (5, 4) rnds.

DEC RND: Keeping in patt, work to 2 sts before m, ssk, sl m, k2, sl m, k2tog, work to end—2 sts dec'd.

Work 7 (5, 4) rnds even in patt. Rep the last 8 (6, 5) rnds 12 (18, 22) more times—48 sts rem. Work even as established until sleeve measures 15¼" (16, 16)" (38.5 [40.5, 40.5]cm) from pick-up rnd, or 6" (15 cm) less than desired total length, changing to dpn when there are too few sts to fit comfortably on cir needle.

INC RND: Work in rib as established and at the same time inc 1 st in each purl section by working p1, M1 pwise (see Glossary), p1—60 sts.

Cont with one strand each of MC1, MC2, and CC held tog in k2, p3 rib for 6" (15 cm). BO all sts in patt.

FINISHING

Weave in loose ends. Lightly steam-press, taking care not to flatted the ribs.

Neckband

With one strand each of MC1 and MC2 held tog, shorter cir needle, and RS facing, pick up and knit 104 sts evenly spaced along neck edge. Work even in k2, p2 rib to match upper body for 10 rows. BO all sts. Fold neckband to WS and with yarn threaded on a tapestry needle, sew in place.

If desired, sew optional fur collar to the neckband. Sew buttons to left front, opposite buttonholes.

sugar

This cardigan is modeled after a sweater worked in garter stitch punctuated with narrow two-stitch cables that my Aunt Ella obtained by trading sugar coupons during World War II. Ella's sweater had ribbed edges, but I chose to decrease one stitch in each panel to taper the lower edge. Instead of increasing stitches along the seam of the sleeves, I placed them between the cables, which make the stripes between the cables taper from the wrist to the upper arm. The two-stitch cables create an interesting texture pattern and prevent the stockinette-stitch ribs from bulging against the garter-stitch background.

FINISHED SIZE
About 36 (39¾)" (91.5 [101] cm) bust circumference, buttoned. Sweater shown measures 36" (91.5 cm).

YARN
About 200 (250) grams of a main color (MC1) of laceweight (#0 Lace) yarn and about 200 (250) grams of a main color (MC2) of fingering-weight (#1 Super Fine) yarn, used held together.

Shown here: **Wool 1** (100% wool; 340 yd [311 m]/50 g): #0 natural (MC1), 4 (5) skeins. **Alpaca 2** (50% merino, 50% alpaca; 270 yd [247 m]/50 g): #2105 light gray heather (MC2), 4 (5) skeins.

NEEDLES
Size U.S. 2 (3 mm): 24" (60 cm) circular (cir). Adjust needle size if necessary to obtain the correct gauge.

NOTIONS
Markers (m); stitch holders; tapestry needle; eleven ½" (1.3 cm) buttons.

GAUGE
26 stitches and 45 rows = 4" (10 cm) in pattern stitch with one strand of each yarn held together.

NOTE
+ Work with one strand each of MC1 and MC2 held together throughout.

STITCH GUIDE
RT (worked over 2 sts)

K2tog but leave on left needle, knit the first st again, then slip both sts off left needle.

GAUGE SWATCH

With one strand each of MC1 and MC2 held tog, CO 21 sts.

ROWS 1 AND 3: (WS) Sl 1 purlwise with yarn in front (pwise wyf), k5, *p2, k4; rep from * 1 more time, p2, k1.

ROW 2: (RS) Knit.

ROW 4: K1, *RT (see Stitch Guide), k4; rep from * 2 more times, k2.

Rep Rows 1–4 of cable twist patt (see Stitch Guide) 2 more times, then work Row 1 once again.

BUTTONHOLE ROW: (RS; Row 2 of patt) K5, M1 (see Glossary), k6, M1, k4, BO 2 sts, k3—5 garter sts between cables.

Work WS Row 3 of patt, working inc'd sts in garter st and using the backward-loop method (see Glossary) to CO 2 sts over gap formed on previous row to complete buttonhole—23 sts. Work Row 4 of patt, then work Rows 1–4 two more times, then work Row 1 once more.

BUTTONHOLE ROW: (RS; Row 2 of patt) K5, M1, k7, M1, k5, BO 2 sts, k3—6 garter sts between cables.

Work Row 3 of patt, working inc'd sts in garter st and using the backward-loop method to CO 2 sts over gap formed on previous row to complete buttonhole—25 sts. Work Row 4 of patt, then work Rows 1–4 two more times.

Block as described on page 33.

BODY

With one strand each of MC1 and MC2 held tog, CO 228 (253) sts—62 (68) sts for right front, 104 (117) sts for back, 62 (68) sts for left front.

ROW 1: (WS) Sl 1 pwise with yarn in front (wyf), k6, [p2, k7 (8)] 6 times, place marker (pm) to mark side seam, p2, pm to mark side seam, [k6 (7), p2] 13 times, pm each side of the last 2 purl sts to mark other side seam, [k7 (8), p2] 6 times, k7.

ROW 2: (RS) Sl 2 pwise wyf, knit to end.

ROW 3: Rep Row 1, slipping markers.

ROW 4: Sl 2 pwise wyf, k5, [RT, k7 (8)] 6 times, sl m, RT, sl m, [k6 (7), RT] 13 times, slipping markers each side of RT, [k7 (8), RT] 6 times, k7.

Rep Rows 1–4 once, then work Row 1 once more.

FIRST BUTTONHOLE ROW: (RS; Row 2 of patt) Sl 2 pwise wyf, BO 2 sts, knit to end.

Work Row 3 of patt, using the backward-loop method (see Glossary) to CO 2 sts over gap formed on previous row to complete buttonhole. Work Row 4 of patt, then work Rows 1–4 two more times, then work Row 1 once more.

SECOND BUTTONHOLE ROW: (RS; Row 2 of patt) Sl 2 pwise wyf, BO 2 sts, knit to first marker, sl m, k2, sl m, k3, M1, k96 (108), M1, k3 (4), sl m, k2, sl m, knit to end—106 (119) back sts.

Work 11 rows even in patt, CO 2 sts over buttonhole gap as before.

THIRD BUTTONHOLE ROW: (RS; Row 2 of patt) Sl 2 pwise wyf, BO 2 sts, knit to first marker, sl m, k2, sl m, k12 (13), M1, k80 (90), M1, k12 (14), sl m, k2, sl m, knit to end—108 (121) back sts.

Work 11 rows even in patt, CO 2 sts over buttonhole gap as before.

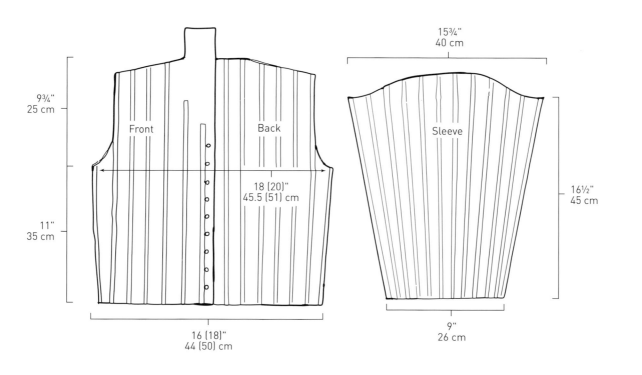

Front

Back

Sleeve

9¾"
25 cm

11"
35 cm

16 (18)"
44 (50) cm

18 (20)"
45.5 (51) cm

15¾"
40 cm

16½"
45 cm

9"
26 cm

FOURTH BUTTONHOLE ROW: (RS; Row 2 of patt) Sl 2 pwise wyf, BO 2 sts, knit to first marker, sl m, k2, sl m, k21 (23), M1, k64 (72), M1, k21 (24), sl m, k2, sl m, knit to end—110 (123) back sts.

Work 11 rows even in patt, CO 2 sts over buttonhole gap as before.

FIFTH BUTTONHOLE ROW: (RS; Row 2 of patt) Sl 2 pwise wyf, BO 2 sts, knit to first marker, sl m, k2, sl m, k30 (33), M1, k48 (54), M1, k30 (34), sl m, k2, sl m, knit to end—112 (125) back sts.

Work 11 rows even in patt, CO 2 sts over buttonhole gap as before.

SIXTH BUTTONHOLE ROW: (RS; Row 2 of patt) Sl 2 pwise wyf, BO 2 sts, knit to first marker, sl m, k2, sl m, k39 (43), M1, k32 (36), M1, k39 (44), sl m, k2, sl m, knit to end—114 (127) back sts.

Work 11 rows even in patt, CO 2 sts over buttonhole gap as before.

SEVENTH BUTTONHOLE ROW: (RS; Row 2 of patt) Sl 2 pwise wyf, BO 2 sts, knit to first marker, sl m, k2, sl m, k48 (53), M1, k16 (18), M1, k48 (54), sl m, k2, sl m, knit to end—116 (129) back sts.

Work 11 rows even in patt, CO 2 sts over buttonhole gap as before.

EIGHTH BUTTONHOLE ROW: (RS; Row 2 of patt) Sl 2 pwise wyf, BO 2 sts, knit to first marker, sl m, k2, sl m, k57 (63), M1, k57 (64), sl m, k2, sl m, knit to end—117 (130) back sts; 241 (266) sts total.

Cont even in established patt until piece measures 11" (28 cm) from CO, ending with WS Row 3 (1) of patt.

Divide for Fronts and Back

(RS; Row 4 [2] of patt) Sl 2 pwise wyf, work in patt to first marker, remove marker, k1, slip the last 62 (68) sts worked to holder for right front, k1, remove marker, work in patt to next marker, remove marker, k1, slip the rem 62 (68) unworked sts to holder for left front—117 (130) sts rem for back.

Back

Work 117 (130) back sts even for 1 WS row.

Shape Armholes

DEC ROW: (RS; Row 2 [4] of patt) K1, k2tog, work in patt to last 3 sts, ssk, k1—2 sts dec'd.

Rep dec row every other row 6 (7) more times—103 (114) sts rem (there will be a RT and single knit st at each side). Work even until armholes measure 8¼" (21 cm), ending with a WS row.

Shape Shoulders

Mark center 29 (32) sts for back neck. Work short-rows (see page 72) as foll.

SHORT-ROW 1: (RS) Work in patt to last 6 sts, turn work, with WS facing, yo, work to last 6 sts, turn work.

SHORT-ROW 2: (RS) Yo, work to 6 sts before yo made on previous row, turn work, yo, work to 6 sts before yo made on previous row, turn work.

Rep Short-row 2 four (five) more times.

SHORT-ROW 3: (RS) Yo, work 7 (5) sts to neck marker closest to yo made on previous row, turn work, yo, work

29 (32) neck sts to other neck marker, turn work.

NEXT ROW: (RS) Yo, *work to next yo, knit the yo tog with the next st; rep from * across, work to end of row.

NEXT ROW: (WS) *Work in patt to next yo, work yo tog with next st (ssk or ssp as necessary to maintain patt); rep from * across, work to end of row.

Place sts on a holder.

Right Front

Place 62 (68) held right front sts on needle. Work WS Row 1 (3) of patt.

Shape Armhole

NOTE: Buttonholes and decreases are worked at the same time that there are changes in the stitch pattern; read all the way through the next section before proceeding. Cont to work buttonhole rows every 12th row until there are 11 buttonholes total and *at the same time* dec as foll.

DEC ROW: (RS Row 2 [4] of patt) Work in patt to last 3 sts, ssk, k1—1 st dec'd.

Work 1 WS row even. Rep the last 2 rows 6 (7) more times—55 (60) sts rem. *Also at the same time* when armhole measures 4" (10 cm), omit the cable closest to the neck edge and work these sts in garter st instead. When armhole measures 6" (15 cm), omit the next cable closest to the neck edge and work these sts in garter st instead. Work even until armhole measures 8¼" (21 cm), end after a WS row.

Shape Shoulder

SHORT-ROW 1: (RS) Work in patt to last 6 sts, turn work, with WS facing, yo, work to end.

SHORT-ROW 2: (RS) Work to 6 sts before yo made on previous row, turn work, yo, work to end.

Rep Short-row 2 four (five) more times.

SHORT-ROW 3: (RS) Work 18 (19) sts, turn work, yo, work to end.

NEXT ROW: (RS) *Work to next yo, knit the yo tog with the next st; rep from * across, work to end of row.

Work 1 WS row even. Place sts on a holder. Do not cut yarn.

Left Front

Place 62 (68) held left front sts on needle. With RS facing, work Row 4 (2) of patt, then work Row 1 (3) of patt.

Shape Armhole

NOTE: Decreases are worked at the same time that there are changes in the stitch pattern; read all the way through the next section before proceeding.

DEC ROW: (RS; Row 2 [4] of patt) K1, k2tog, work in patt to end—1 st dec'd.

Work 1 WS row even. Rep the last 2 rows 6 (7) more times—55 (60) sts rem. *At the same time* when armhole measures 4" (10 cm), omit the cable closest to the neck edge and work these sts in garter st instead. When armhole measures 6" (15 cm), omit the next cable closest to the neck edge and work these sts in garter st instead. Work even until armhole measures 8¼" (21 cm), ending with a RS row.

Shape Shoulder

SHORT-ROW 1: (WS) Work in patt to last 6 sts, turn work, with RS facing, yo, work to end.

SHORT-ROW 2: (WS) Work to 6 sts before yo made on previous row, turn work, yo, work to end.

Rep Short-row 2 four (five) more times.

SHORT-ROW 3: (WS) Work 18 (19) sts, turn work, yo, work to end.

NEXT ROW: (WS) *Work to next yo, work yo tog with next st (ssk or ssp, keeping in patt); rep from * across, work to end of row.

Work 1 RS row even. Place sts on a holder. Do not cut yarn.

JOIN FRONTS TO BACK AT SHOULDERS

Place 37 (41) sts closest to the armhole edge of the held right front sts on one needle and the corresponding 37 (41) held right back shoulder sts on another needle. Hold the pieces with RS facing tog and use the three-needle method (see Glossary) to BO the sts tog. Rep for left shoulder—18 (19) sts rem for each front neck; 29 (32) sts for back neck.

Neck

Place 18 (19) held right front neck sts onto needle. With RS facing and yarn already attached, work these sts in garter st, slipping the st at the neck edge as established, until neck measures 2½ (2¾)" (6.5 [7] cm), or the same length as corresponding half of back neck. Place sts on a holder. Rep for left front. Place held right front sts on a needle and with RS facing tog, use the three-needle method to BO the front neck sts tog. Place 29 (32) back neck sts onto needle. With RS facing, use a second needle to pick up and knit 29 (32) sts along selvedge edge of front necks. With RS facing tog, use the three-needle method to BO the sts tog.

SLEEVES

With one strand each of MC1 and MC2 held tog, CO 59 sts.

ROWS 1 AND 3: (WS) K1, *p2, k3; rep from * to last 3 sts, p2, k1.

ROW 2: Knit.

ROW 4: K1, *RT, k3; rep from * to last 3 sts, RT, k1.

Rep Rows 1–4 until piece measures 4" (10 cm) from CO, end after WS row 3 of patt.

INC ROW 1: (RS; Row 4 of patt) K1, *RT, k1, M1, k2; rep from * to last 3 sts, RT, k1—70 sts.

Working inc'd sts in garter st, work even in patt until piece measures 8" (20.5 cm) from CO, ending with Row 3 of patt.

INC ROW 2: (RS; Row 4 of patt) K1, *RT, k2, M1, k2; rep from * to last 3 sts, RT, k1—81 sts.

Working inc'd sts in garter st, work even in patt until piece measures 11½" (30 cm) from CO, ending with Row 3 of patt.

INC ROW 3: (RS; Row 4 of patt) K1, *RT, k2, M1, k3; rep from * to last 3 sts, RT, k1—92 sts.

Working inc'd sts in garter st, work even in patt until piece measures 15¾" (40 cm) from CO, ending with Row 3 of patt.

INC ROW 4: (RS; Row 4 of patt) K1, *RT, k3, M1, k3; rep from * to last 3 sts, RT, k1—103 sts.

Work even in patt until piece measures 16½" (42 cm) from CO, or desired length to armhole, end after a WS row.

Shape Cap

(RS) BO 10 sts at beg of next 2 rows, then BO 3 sts at beg of the foll 18 rows—29 sts rem. BO all sts.

FINISHING

Block to measurements. With yarn threaded on a tapestry needle, use the mattress st (see Glossary) to sew sleeve caps into armholes. Sew sleeve and side seams. Sew buttons to left front, aligning them with the outer edge of the buttonholes.

technique: measuring gauge

Most knitters consider their knitting to be "completely normal," but in reality, the size of swatches worked by two different knitters can be quite different, even if they use the same needles and yarn—and that can affect the finished size of a garment. For this reason, I begin every design in this book with a substantial gauge swatch. It is imperative that you knit the gauge swatch before beginning a garment. I recommend the needle size I used, but it's quite possible that you will need larger or smaller needles to produce the same gauge.

For an example, take a look at Knit & Purl on page 64. This sweater is sized for both men and boys. But rather than changing the number of stitches, the sizing is achieved by using different yarns and needles—one combination produces a large gauge and the other produces a small gauge. Keep this in mind whenever you decide to substitute yarns. In these cases, swatching is even more important.

After you've knitted the swatch, wash it in cold water. Press out the extra water in a hand towel and block the swatch on a damp towel, pinning it to the correct size with rustproof pins. This is easiest if you place a checked cloth over the towel so you can align the sides precisely. When the swatch is completely dry, remove the pins and measure the gauge. If your swatch measures the same as specified in the pattern, you can be assured that your garment will be the right size. If your swatch is smaller than specified, work it again with larger needles; if it is larger, work it again with smaller needles.

The finished garment pieces can be blocked the same way as the swatch. Lay towels on a carpet and pin pieces to the correct measurements. Laying the pieces flat keeps the knit structure even. If you prefer to block by steam-pressing, lightly steam the garment on the wrong side under a damp cloth.

fisherman

The edgings on this simple ribbed sweater resemble a woven twill pattern. It is worked by alternating two knit stitches with two slipped stitches. The repeat is shifted one stitch every row to create a diagonal pattern, which pulls in and stabilizes the edges. For the sweater shown, I used three yarns of similar neutral colors held together throughout. The body and sleeves are worked separately from the lower edges to the armholes, then they are joined, and the seamless yoke is worked in a single piece to the neck.

FINISHED SIZE
About 42 (44½)" (106.5 [113] cm) chest circumference. Sweater shown measures 44½" (113 cm).

YARN
About 300 (350) grams each of three colors (MC1, MC2, and MC3) of fingering-weight (#1 Super Fine) yarn used held together.

Shown here: **Viscolin** (50% viscose, 50% linen; 202 yd [185 m]/50 g): #1000 natural (MC1), 6 (7) skeins. **Bomulin** (75% cotton, 25% linen; 228 yd [208 m]/50 g): #1000 natural (MC2), 6 (7) skeins. **Bomuld** (100% cotton; 228 yd [208 m]/50 g): #13 natural (MC3), 6 (7) skeins.

NEEDLES
Size U.S. 6 (4 mm): straight and 24" (60 cm) circular (cir). Adjust needle size if necessary to obtain the correct gauge.

NOTIONS
Markers (m); stitch holders; tapestry needle.

GAUGE
18 stitches and 28 rows = 4" (10 cm) in k5, p5 rib pattern with one strand each of MC1, MC2, and MC3 held together, stretched; 21 stitches and 28 rows = 4" (10 cm) in charted pattern.

NOTES
+ Work with one strand each of MC1, MC2, and MC3 held together throughout.
+ The sweater shown on pages 39 and 40 was worked with one strand each of Viscolin (in #43 olive) and Highland (in almond green) held together.

GAUGE SWATCH

With one strand each of MC1, MC2, and MC3 held tog, CO 20 sts. Work in k5, p5 rib for 22 rows. Knitting the first and last st of every row for edge sts, work the center 18 sts according to Rows 1–4 of Woven Knitting chart for 12 rows, ending with Row 4. With RS facing, BO all sts knitwise. Block as described on page 33.

BODY

With cir needle and one strand each of MC1, MC2, and MC3 held tog, CO 189 (201) sts. Place marker (pm) and join for working in rnds, being careful not to twist sts. Rnd begs at side "seam."

RND 1: *K2, sl 2 pwise wyf; rep from * to last st, k1.

RND 2: *K1, sl 2 pwise wyf, k1; rep from * to last st, k1.

RND 3: *Sl 2 pwise wyf, k2; rep from * to last st, sl 1 pwise wyf.

RND 4: *Sl 1 pwise wyf, k2, sl pwise wyf; rep from * to last st, sl 1 pwise wyf.

Woven Knitting

- ☐ knit on RS; purl on WS
- ☐ knit on RS; knit on WS
- ☒ sl 1 with yarn in front on RS; sl 1 with yarn in back on WS
- ☐ pattern repeat

Rep Rnds 1–4 until piece measures 1½ (2)" (3.8 [5] cm) from CO, or desired length. Inc 1 (dec 1) st at end of last rnd—190 (200) sts. Place a second marker (of another color) after 95 (100) sts to mark the other side "seam."

NEXT RND: *K5, p5; rep from *.

Work in rib as established until piece measures 13¾ (15¾)" (35 [40] cm) from CO or desired length to armhole. Place 15 (16) sts at each side "seam" on holder for underarm, taking 5 (8) sts from before each marker and 10 (8) sts from after each marker—160 (168) sts rem; 80 (84) sts each for front and back. Set aside.

SLEEVES

With straight needles and one strand each of MC1, MC2, and MC3 held tog, CO 54 sts. Work Rows 1–4 of Woven Knitting chart as foll:

ROW 1: (RS) K2, *sl 2 pwise wyf, k2; rep from * to end.

ROW 2: (WS) K1, p1, sl 1 pwise wyb, *p2, sl 2 pwise wyb; rep from * to last 3 sts, p2, k1.

ROW 3: K2, *k2, sl 2 pwise wyf; rep from * to last 4 sts, k4.

ROW 4: K1, p2, *sl 2 pwise wyb, p2; rep from * to last 3 sts, sl 1 pwise wyb, p1, k1.

Rep Rows 1–4 until piece measures 1½ (2)" (3.8 [5] cm) from CO.

NEXT ROW: K2, *k5, p5; rep from * to last 2 sts, k2.

NEXT ROW: (WS) K1, p1, *k5, p5; rep from * to last 2 sts, p1, k1.

INC ROW: (RS) K2, M1 (see Glossary), work in patt to last 2 sts, M1, k2—2 sts inc'd.

Rep inc row every 8th row 10 (12) more times, working inc'd sts into rib patt—76 (80) sts. Work even if necessary until piece measures 15¾ (18½)" (40 [47] cm) from CO, or desired length to armhole, ending with a WS row. Place sts on holder. Make a second sleeve to match.

Size Medium

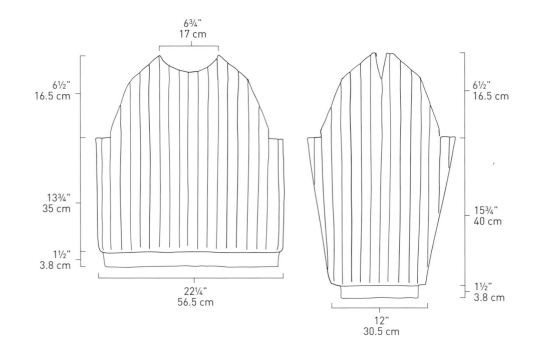

6¾"
17 cm

6½"
16.5 cm

6½"
16.5 cm

13¾"
35 cm

15¾"
40 cm

1½"
3.8 cm

1½"
3.8 cm

22¼"
56.5 cm

12"
30.5 cm

Size Large

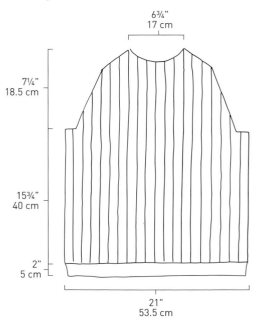
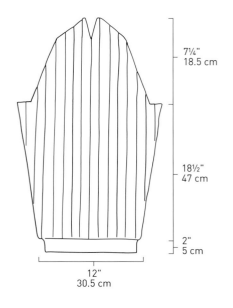

6¾"
17 cm

7¼"
18.5 cm

7¼"
18.5 cm

15¾"
40 cm

18½"
47 cm

2"
5 cm

2"
5 cm

21"
53.5 cm

12"
30.5 cm

JOIN BODY AND SLEEVES

With RS facing, place 8 sts on each side of sleeve on a holder and join rem sleeve sts with body sts as foll: slip all rem sts from front, back, and sleeves to cir needle; pm between each piece to mark raglan seam—280 (296) sts total (60 [64] sts for each sleeve, 80 [84] sts each for front and back).

Size medium only

Work in established rib for 1¼" (3 cm).

Size large only

Work in established rib for 1 rnd.

DEC RND: Keeping in patt, *work to 3 sts before m, ssk or p2tog as necessary to maintain patt, k1, slip marker (sl m), k1, k2tog or p2tog as necessary to maintain patt; rep from * 3 more times—8 sts dec'd.

Rep dec rnd every 3rd rnd 10 (12) more times—192 sts rem. Work dec rnd every rnd 2 more times—176 sts rem (54 sts each for back and front; 34 sts for each sleeve). Place a marker between the center 2 sts on each sleeve and on each side of the center 10 sts on front.

RND 1: Work dec rnd and *at the same time* *work to center sleeve marker, sl m, k2tog; rep from * once—166 sts rem (52 sts each for front and back; 31 sts for each sleeve).
RND 2: Work dec rnd in patt to 10 marked center front sts, BO marked sts removing marker, work to end of rnd as for dec rnd—148 sts rem (20 sts for each side of front neck; 50 sts for back; 29 sts for each sleeve).

Turn work and cont back and forth in rows as foll.

ROW 3: (WS) Keeping in patt, BO 3 sts, *work to 3 sts before m, k2tog or ssp as necessary to maintain patt, p1, sl m, p1, k2tog or p2tog as necessary to maintain patt; rep from * 3 more times, work to end—137 sts rem.
ROW 4: (RS) BO 3 sts, work to end as for dec rnd—126 sts rem (15 sts for each front; 46 sts for back; 25 sts for each sleeve).
ROW 5: Rep Row 3—115 sts rem.
ROW 6: BO 3 sts, work as for dec rnd and *at the same time* *work to 2 sts before center sleeve m, ssk, sl m; rep from * once—102 sts rem (10 sts for each front; 42 sts for back; 20 sts for each sleeve).

Remove center sleeve markers and cont working decs at each raglan marker and *at the same time* BO 2 sts at beg of next 2 rows, then BO 1 st at beg of next 4 rows—46 sts rem (0 sts for each front; 30 sts for back; 8 sts for each sleeve). Work 1 WS row even.

FINISHING

Neckband

(RS) Knit across all sts, then pick up and knit 35 sts along front neck BO—81 sts total. Work Rnds 1–4 of Woven Knitting chart as for lower edge of body until piece measures 1½" (4 cm) from pick-up rnd. Loosely BO all sts.

Place 16 held sts of one underarm on one needle and the held sts of the corresponding sleeve onto another needle. Hold the sts with RS facing tog and use the three-needle method (see Glossary) to BO the sts tog. Rep for the other underarm.

With yarn threaded on a tapestry needle, use the mattress st (see Glossary) to sew sleeve seams. Weave in loose ends. Block to measurements.

technique: knitting in the round

When you knit in the round, all of the stitches are worked in the same direction with the right side of the fabric always facing you. This allows you to work stockinette stitch without having to purl any stitches. To accommodate different numbers of stitches, circular needles come in a variety of lengths from about 12" (30.5 cm) to 40" (101.5 cm). If there are too few stitches in your project to fit comfortably on the shortest circular needle you have, you can use a set of double-pointed needles instead.

To work on double-pointed needles, divide the stitches onto three or four needles and use the fourth or fifth needle to knit with. Keep in mind that the stitches at the boundaries between needles can be loose and cause a visual line (called a ladder) to show in the knitting. To prevent this from happening, periodically shift the stitches on the needles so the boundaries aren't always in the same place.

Whether you use circular or double-pointed needles, there will be a little "jog" where one round begins and the previous one ends. For this reason, always position the beginning of round along the side seam of a garment where the jog will be least visible.

monk

I've named this sweater Monk in honor of the hood and tassel. The diagonal stripe ribbing is made by shifting the rib over by one stitch on each row. The triangles at the sweater's lower edge are worked in intarsia. This sweater, sized for both children and adults, is easy to lengthen because there is no armhole shaping. If you want it to be very long, I suggest that you omit the intarsia triangles and continue the diagonal stripes all the way to the lower edge.

FINISHED SIZE
About 36 (41¼)" (91.5 [105] cm) chest circumference. Sized to fit 10-12 years (woman's medium). White sweater shown measures 41¼" (105 cm). Blue sweater shown measures 36" (91.5 cm).

YARN
About 150 (200) grams of a main color (MC1) of laceweight (#0 Lace) yarn, 150 (200) grams of a main color (MC2) of fingering-weight (#1 Super Fine) yarn, 200 (250) grams of a main color (MC3) of another laceweight yarn, and 50 grams of a contrasting color (CC) of fingering-weight yarn.

Shown here: **Wool 1** (100% wool; 340 yd [311 m]/50 g): #2s light gray heather or #10s light blue heather (MC1), 3 (4) skeins. **Alpaca 2** (50% merino, 50% alpaca; 270 yd [247 m]/50 g): #2105 light gray heather or #019 light blue (MC2), 3 (4) skeins; #500 black (CC), 1 (1) skein (used double). **Alpaca 1** (100% alpaca; 437 yd [400 m]/50 g): #2105 light gray heather or #019 light blue (MC3), 4 (5) skeins.

NEEDLES
Size U.S. 7 (4.5 mm): 24" (60 cm) circular (cir). Adjust needle size if necessary to obtain the correct gauge.

NOTIONS
Stitch holders; tapestry needle.

GAUGE
18 stitches and 25 rows = 4" (10 cm) in k3, p3 rib pattern with one strand each of MC1, MC2, and MC3 held together.

NOTES
+ Work with one strand each of MC1, MC2, and MC3 held together throughout for the main color and two strands of CC held together for the contrast color.

+ Work each color section with separate balls of yarn, twisting the yarns around each other at color changes in the intarsia method of knitting (see page 49).

+ Work a chain stitch selvedge by slipping the first stitch of every row purlwise (pwise) with yarn in front (wyf).

+ The gauge swatch can be used for one of the side triangles.

GAUGE SWATCH

CO 3 sts with one strand each of MC1, MC2, and MC3 held tog (designated MC), then CO 21 sts with two strands of CC held tog; then CO 9 more sts with different balls of MC—33 sts total. Work Triangle chart (see page 47) as foll, twisting yarns at color changes (see Notes).

ROW 1: (WS) With MC, sl 1 pwise wyf, p2, k3, p3, change to CC, *k3, p3; rep from * to last 3 CC sts, k3, change to MC, p2, k1.

ROW 2: (RS) Sl 1 pwise wyf, k3, change to CC and work in ribbing and colors as established, working 1 less st in CC.

Cont as charted, working 1 more MC st each row until no CC sts rem. Cont working Triangle chart with MC only until all rows of chart have been worked. Place all sts on a holder.

Block as described on page 33. If the swatch has the correct gauge, you can put the sts on a holder instead of binding off and use it to begin the sweater.

FRONT

Side Triangles

Use gauge swatch as the first side triangle.

Make another triangle as for gauge swatch, but reverse shaping as foll: CO 9 sts with MC, then CO 21 sts with CC, then CO 3 sts with different balls of MC—33 sts total. Work Reverse Triangle chart as foll, twisting yarns at color changes (see Notes) as foll.

ROW 1: (WS) Sl 1 pwise wyf, p2, change to CC, *k3, p3; rep from * to last 3 CC sts, k3, change to MC, p3, k3, p2, k1.

ROW 2: (RS) Sl 1 pwise, k2, p3, k3, change to CC and work in ribbing but change to MC 1 st sooner than on previous row, knit the last st.

Cont as established, working 1 more MC st each row until no CC sts rem. Cont working Reverse Triangle chart until all rows of chart have been worked. Place sts on a holder.

Center Section

With MC, CO 21 (33) sts.

ROW 1: (WS) Sl 1, p2, k3, *p3, k3; rep from * to last 3 sts, p2, k1.

ROW 2: Sl 1, k2, *p3, k3; rep from *.

Rep Rows 1 and 2 until piece measures same length as side triangles. Place sts on a holder.

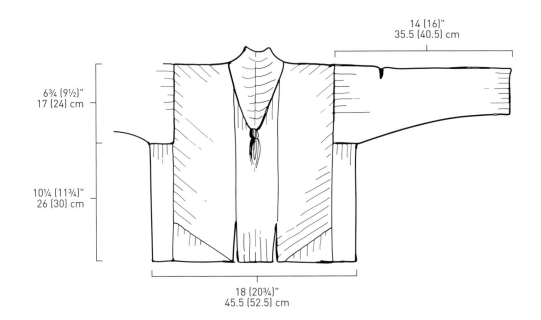

14 (16)"
35.5 (40.5) cm

6¾ (9½)"
17 (24) cm

10¼ (11¾)"
26 (30) cm

18 (20¾)"
45.5 (52.5) cm

JOIN TRIANGLES AND CENTER

Slip sts from holders with RS facing as foll: 33 sts from second (reverse) triangle, 21 (33) sts from center section, 33 sts from first (gauge swatch) triangle—87 (99) sts total.

DEC ROW: (RS) Join yarn, work to last 3 sts of second (reverse) triangle, ssk, work another ssk over last st of second triangle and first st of center section, k2tog, work in patt to last 3 sts of center section, ssk, work k2tog over last st of center section and first st of first (gauge swatch) triangle, k2tog, work in patt to end—6 sts dec'd; 81 (93) sts rem.

SET-UP ROW: (WS) Rep the last 10 rows of the chart only, work 33 sts according to Triangle chart, work the next 15 (27) sts in rib as established, work rem 33 sts according to Reverse Triangle chart.

Work in patt as established until piece measures 10¼ (11¾)" (26 [30] cm) from CO or desired length to armholes, ending with a WS row.

Shape Armholes

BO 8 sts at beg of next 2 rows—65 (77) sts rem. Work as established until armholes measure 4¼ (5½)" (11 [14] cm), ending with a WS row.

Shape Neck

(RS) Keeping in patt, work 32 (38) sts, join new yarn and BO center st, work to end—32 (38) sts each side. Working each side separately, work a chain st selvedge (see Notes) at each neck edge as foll: Work in patt to 1 st before divide, k1; on other side, sl 1 wyf, work to end in patt. Work in patt until split measures 2½ (4)" (6 [10] cm) and armholes measure 6¾ (9½)" (17 [24] cm). Place sts on holders.

BACK

Work as for front, omitting slit at neck, until armholes measure 6¾ (9½)" (17 [24] cm)—65 (77) sts.

JOIN FRONTS TO BACK AT SHOULDERS

Place 22 held right front shoulder sts (diagonal stripes) on one needle and 22 corresponding right back shoulder sts on another needle. Hold the pieces with RS facing tog and use the three-needle method (see Glossary) to BO the sts tog. Rep for left shoulder.

HOOD

Place 10 (16) right front rib sts, 21 (33) back neck sts, and 10 (16) left front rib sts on cir needle—41 (65) sts total.

SET-UP ROW: (RS) Join yarn and work in patt across right front sts to right shoulder, use the backward-loop method (see Glossary) to CO 3 sts, work in patt across back to left shoulder, use the backward-loop method to CO 3 sts, work in patt to end—47 (71) sts.

Work 4 more rows as established, working CO sts in rib and ending with a WS row. Place marker (pm) each side of center 3 sts.

INC ROW 1: (RS) Work in patt to m, sl m, M1 pwise (see Glossary), p3, M1P, sl m, work to end in patt—2 sts inc'd; 5 rev St st sts at center.

Work 3 (5) rows even as established, ending with a WS row.

INC ROW 2: (RS) Work in patt to m, sl m, M1P, p2, k1, p2, M1P, sl m, work to end in patt—2 sts inc'd; 7 sts between markers; 51 (75) sts total.

Work 3 (5) rows even as established, ending with a WS row. Replace markers on each side of center st.

INC ROW 3: (RS) Work in patt to m, M1 (see Glossary) or M1P as necessary to maintain patt, sl m, k1, sl m, M1 or M1P as necessary to maintain patt, work to end in patt—2 sts inc'd.

Work 3 (5) rows even, ending with a WS row. Rep the last 4 (6) rows 8 (5) more times—69 (87) sts. Work even in patt until piece measures 10 (11)" (25.5 [28] cm), or desired length. Place the first 34 (43) sts on one needle and the rem 36 (45) sts on another needle. Holding the piece with RS facing tog, and beg by slipping the first st on the needle that has more sts, use the three-needle method to BO all sts.

Triangle

Reverse Triangle

□ with MC, knit on RS; purl on WS

⊡ with MC, purl on RS; knit on WS

▨ with CC, knit on RS; purl on WS

▣ with CC, purl on RS; knit on WS

SLEEVES

With MC and RS facing, pick up and knit 63 (87) sts evenly spaced around the armhole (do not include 8 BO sts at each side).

NEXT ROW: (WS) K1 (edge st), k2, p3, *k3, p3; rep from * to last 3 sts, k2, k1 (edge st).

Knitting the first st of every row, work in rib as established until piece measures 1½" (3.8 cm) from pick-up row, ending with a WS row.

DEC ROW: (RS) K1, ssk or p2tog as necessary to maintain patt, work in patt to last 3 sts, k2tog or p2tog as necessary to maintain patt, k1—2 sts dec'd.

Dec 1 st each end of needle in this manner every 4th row 14 (18) more times—33 (49) sts rem. Work even if necessary until piece measures 14 (16)" (35.5 [40.5] cm) from pick-up row, or desired total length. BO all sts in patt.

Work a second sleeve to match, but insert a pocket when piece measures 4 (4¾)" (10 [12] cm) from pick-up row as foll: Keeping in patt, work to center 9 sts, place these 9 sts on a holder, use the backward-loop method to CO 9 sts over the gap, work to end.

FINISHING

Weave in loose ends. Block to measurements.

Pocket Lining

Place the 9 held pocket sts onto needle. Join CC and work even in St st until lining measures 2½" (6.5 cm). BO all sts. With yarn threaded on a tapestry needle, sew lining to WS of sleeve.

Tassel

With CC, make an 8" (20.5 cm) tassel (see Glossary). With yarn threaded on a tapestry needle, sew tassel to top of hood.

technique: intarsia knitting

Intarsia is a method of working isolated areas of color. Separate balls of yarn are used for each section, or block, of color. The most important thing to remember when knitting intarsia is that the yarns need to be twisted around each other at the color changes. Otherwise, there will be gaps (holes) between the different colors of knitting.

To practice intarsia knitting, you will need needles and one ball each of a dark- and light-colored yarn. With the dark yarn, cast on 4 stitches. With the light yarn, cast on 4 more stitches onto the same needle (Figure 1). Turn the work around to work the first wrong-side row. Work in stockinette stitch as follows:

Wrong-Side (Purl) Rows
With the light yarn, purl the 4 light stitches, then drop the light yarn to front (purl side) of the work. Pick up the dark yarn from underneath the light yarn (Figure 2), then use it to purl the 4 dark stitches.

Right-Side (Knit) Rows
With the dark yarn, knit the 4 dark stitches, then drop the dark yarn to the back (purl side) of the work. Pick up the light yarn over the dark yarn (Figure 3), then knit the next 4 stitches with the light yarn.

Repeat these two rows, always dropping the old color to the wrong (purl) side of the work and always picking up the new color over the old. Pull gently on the new color before knitting the first stitch to close the gap between the two colors.

If a pattern calls for many blocks of color in the same row, wind a separate butterfly of yarn for each section to prevent the yarns from tangling on each other. To make a butterfly, wind the yarn into a figure-eight around your thumb and little finger the desired number of times. To finish, wind the yarn around the center of the bundle a couple of times, then secure the tail on one of these center wraps (Figure 4). Pull the working end from the center (shown with an arrow) as needed.

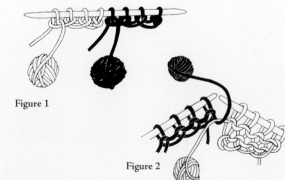

Figure 1

Figure 2

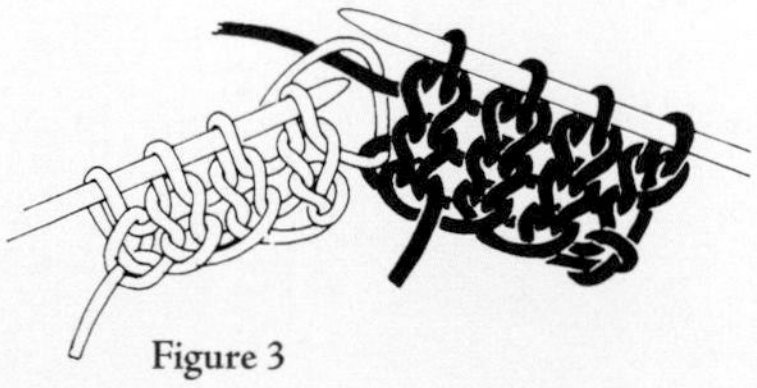

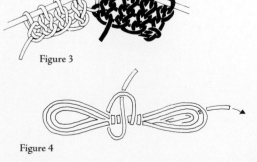

Figure 3

Figure 4

elf

FINISHED SIZE
About 24¼" (61.5 cm) chest
circumference. To fit newborn to 1 year.

YARN
About 100 grams each of a light color
(L1) and a dark color (D1) of laceweight
(#0 Lace) yarn and about 100 grams
each of a light color (L2) and a dark
color (D2) of another laceweight yarn.

Shown here: **Alpaca 1** (100% alpaca;
437 yd [400 m]/50 g): #2105 light gray
heather (L1) and #402 charcoal (D1),
2 skeins each. **Wool 1** (100% wool;
340 yd [311 m]/50 g): #2s light gray
heather (L2) and #47 steel gray (D2),
2 skeins each. Small amounts of four
(or more) colors as desired. *Note:* The
bright turquoise and navy blue shown
have been discontinued.

NEEDLES
Body—size U.S. 4 (3.5 mm) straight and
24" (60 cm) circular (cir). Ribbing—size
U.S. 2 (3 mm). Spare needle for three-
needle bind-off. Adjust needle size if
necessary to obtain the correct gauge.

NOTIONS
Markers (m); stitch holders; tapestry
needle; 12" (30 cm) zipper.

Elf is a one-piece outfit for the littlest one. This
design is worked in the intarsia technique of
working each block of color with a different ball
of yarn and twisting the yarn around each other
at color changes to prevent holes from forming.
The front yoke is decorated with vertical bands of
contrasting colors added in duplicate stitch after
the knitting is complete. The edges on the sleeves,
legs, and hood are also trimmed with a contrasting
color. The garment fastens with a zipper.

GAUGE
25 stitches and 32 rows = 4" (10 cm)
in stockinette stitch with one strand
each of L1 and L2 or D1 and D2 held
together.

NOTES
+ Work with one strand each of L1 and
  L2 held together for light color and
  one strand each of D1 and D2 held
  together for the dark color.

+ Use the intarsia technique of
  twisting the yarns around each other
  at color changes to prevent holes
  (see page 49).

+ The sample garment photographed
  flat on pages 53 and 54 has
  the colors reversed from the
  instructions.

+ Use fingering-weight (#1 Super Fine)
  yarn to make a larger size.

GAUGE SWATCH

NOTE: The swatch shown has a horizontal color stripe that is not specified in the garment instructions here. With one strand each of L1 and L2 held tog and larger needles, CO 11 sts, then with one strand each of D1 and D2 held tog, CO 11 more sts onto the same needle—22 sts total.

ROW 1: (WS) With both dark yarns, k1, p10, with both light yarns, p10, k1.

ROW 2: (RS) With both light yarns, k11, with both dark yarns, k11.

Rep these 2 rows 6 more times—14 rows total. Reverse the color sequence, working light over dark and dark over light for 14 more rows. BO all sts.

Block as described on page 33. Work contrasting colors in duplicate st (see Glossary) as shown in photograph and chart opposite.

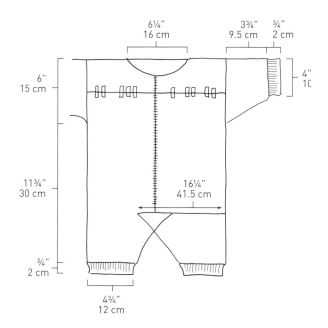

LEGS (MAKE 2)

With two strands of your choice of CC held tog and smaller needles, CO 58 sts.

SET-UP ROW: (WS) With one strand each of D1 and D2 held tog, k1, p1; rep from * until a total of 29 sts have been worked, change to one strand each of L1 and L2 held tog and cont in rib as established to end of row.

Work in rib and colors as established until piece measures ¾" (2 cm) from CO. Change to larger needles and St st.

INC ROW: (RS) K1 (edge st), M1 (see Glossary), knit in colors as established to last st, M1, k1 (edge st)—2 sts inc'd.

Cont in St st, inc 1 st each end of needle in this manner every RS row 18 more times—96 sts. Purl 1 row. Cut yarn. Place sts on a holder. Make another leg to match, but leave sts on needles.

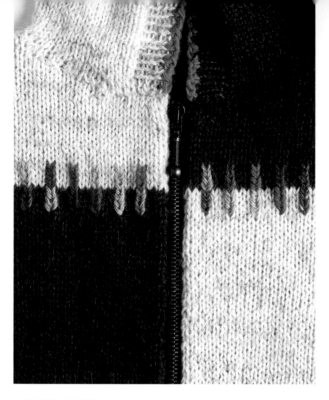

LOWER BODY

With cir needle, RS facing and keeping in color patt as established, join legs as foll: BO 3 sts for center front, work to last 3 sts of first leg, k2tog, k1, place marker (pm) for center back, then work across other leg as foll: k1, ssk, knit to end—187 sts. At beg of the next row (WS), BO 3 sts, purl to end—184 sts rem. BO 2 sts at beg of next 4 rows, then BO 1 st at beg of foll 6 rows (10 sts total dec'd at each front) and *at the same time* dec 1 st each side of center back every RS row as established 9 more times—152 sts rem. Work even in patt until piece measures 11¾" (30 cm) from beg of St st, ending with a WS row.

DIVIDE FOR ARMHOLES

(RS) Keeping in patt, k38 right front sts and place these sts on holder, work next 76 sts for back, place rem 38 left front sts on another holder without working them.

Back

Keeping in patt, work 76 sts back sts even until armholes measure 2¾" (7 cm). Reverse position of dark and light yarns and cont even until armholes measure 6" (15 cm). Place sts on holder.

RIGHT FRONT

Place 38 held right front sts on needle. Beg with a WS row, work even until armhole measures 2¾" (7 cm). Reverse dark and light yarns as for back and cont even until armhole measures 4¼" (11 cm), ending with a WS row.

Shape Neck

At neck edge (beg of RS rows), BO 9 sts once, then BO 3 sts 2 times, then BO 2 sts once, then BO 1 st once—20 sts rem. Work even until armhole measures 6" (15 cm). Place sts on holder.

LEFT FRONT

Place 38 held left front sts on needle. Work even until armhole measures 2¾" (7 cm). Reverse dark and light yarns and cont even until armhole measures 4¼" (11 cm), ending with a RS row.

Shape Neck

At neck edge (beg of WS rows), BO 9 sts once, then BO 3 sts 2 times, then BO 2 sts once, then BO 1 st once—20 sts rem. Work even until armhole measures 6" (15 cm), ending with a RS row.

JOIN FRONTS AND BACK

Place 76 held back sts on a needle. Hold the left front and back pieces with RS facing tog and use the three-needle method (see Glossary) to BO 20 shoulder sts tog. Place the next 36 sts from back on holder for back neck. Rep three-needle bind-off for other shoulder.

SLEEVES

With dark yarn, larger needles, and beg at base of right armhole, pick up and knit 35 sts evenly spaced along back armhole to top of shoulder, change to light yarn and pick up and knit 35 sts evenly spaced along front armhole—70 sts total. Keeping in color patt as established, work 5 rows even.

Duplicate Stitch

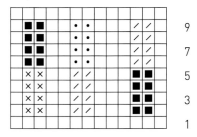

Use various contrasting colors of your choosing (shown by different symbols) for duplicate stitches.

DEC ROW: (RS) K1, k2tog, work in patt to last 3 sts, ssk, k1—2 sts dec'd.

Dec 1 st each end of needle every 6th row in this manner 4 more times—60 sts rem. Work even until piece measures about 3¾" (9.5 cm) or desired length to ribbing, ending with a WS row.

NEXT ROW: Dec 16 sts evenly spaced—44 sts rem.

Cuff

With smaller needles, work in k1, p1 rib for ¾" (2 cm). Change to two strands of your choice of CC held tog and work 1 row in rib as established. BO all sts in patt.

HOOD

With dark yarn, larger needles, RS facing, and beg ¾" (2 cm) from center front, pick up and knit 18 sts to shoulder, work across 18 back sts, change to light yarn and work rem 18 back neck sts, then pick up and knit 18 sts along left front neck, ending ¾" (2 cm) from center front edge—72 sts total. Keeping in color patt as established, work in short-rows (see page 72) as foll.

SHORT-ROW 1: (WS) P5, turn work, yo, knit to end.
SHORT-ROW 2: Purl to yo, p2tog (yo with foll st), p4, turn work, yo, knit to end.
NEXT ROW: Work across all sts, working yo tog with the foll st.
SHORT-ROW 3: (RS) K5, turn work, yo, purl to end.
SHORT-ROW 4: Knit to yo, k2tog (yo with foll st), k4, turn work, yo, purl to end.
NEXT ROW: Work across all sts, working yo tog with the foll st.

Work even for 4" (10 cm), ending with a WS row.

INC ROW: (RS) Knit to 1 st before color change, M1, k2, M1, knit to end—2 sts inc'd.

Rep inc row every RS row 14 more times—102 sts; hood measures about 8" (20.5 cm) at center back. Place the light sts on one needle and the dark sts on another needle, hold the pieces with RS facing tog, and use the three-needle method to BO the sts tog.

Edging

Maintaining the same colors, with smaller needles and RS facing, pick up and knit about 10 sts for every 2" (5 cm) around front opening—80 sts total. Work in k1, p1 rib for ¾" (2 cm). Change to two strands of CC of your choice held tog and work 1 row in rib as established. BO all sts in patt.

FINISHING

With yarn threaded on a tapestry needle, sew the hood edgings to the top of the neck opening. Steam-press garment carefully on WS. Sew zipper (see Glossary) to front opening. With 2 strands of CC threaded on a tapestry needle, use the duplicate st (see Glossary) to add contrasting bands to fronts as shown on chart above.

Weave in loose ends. Make a pom-pom (see Glossary) and sew to tip of hood, if desired.

elf

55

short jacket

The body and cuffs of this jacket are worked in brioche stitch. Brioche stitch is easy and fun to knit and, because it looks the same on both sides, it forms a reversible fabric. On the other hand, it can be difficult to pick up dropped stitches in this pattern, so pay attention as you knit. The sleeves and front yoke are worked in a combination of knit and purl stitches that create a raised spiral pattern. The back yoke is worked in a basketweave pattern. The neck is finished with a sawtooth edging in a contrasting color, and the jacket fastens with a couple of buttons.

FINISHED SIZE
About 40 (45)" (101.5 [114.5] cm) bust circumference, buttoned. Jacket shown measures 40" (101.5 cm).

YARN
About 250 (300) grams of a main color (MC1) of fingering-weight (#1 Super Fine) yarn and abut 200 (250) grams of a main color (MC2) of laceweight (#0 Lace) yarn, used held together. About 10 grams of a contrasting color (CC) of laceweight yarn, used with four strands held together.

Shown here: **Alpaca 2** (50% merino, 50% alpaca; 270 yd [247 m]/50 g): #201 tan heather (MC1), 5 (6) skeins. **Wool 1** (100% wool; 340 yd [311 m]/50 g): #3s light tan heather (MC2), 4 (5) skeins; #47 steel gray (CC), less than 1 skein.

NEEDLES
Size 4 U.S. (3.5 mm). Adjust needle size if necessary to obtain the correct gauge.

NOTIONS
Stitch holders; tapestry needle; one 1" (2.5 cm) and one ½" x ½" (1.3 x 2 cm) decorative button.

GAUGE
16 stitches and 44 rows = 4" (10 cm) in brioche stitch with one strand each of MC1 and MC2 held together, relaxed; 20 stitches and 29 rows = 4" (10 cm) in basketweave pattern.

NOTES
+ Work with one strand each MC1 and MC2 held together for the body and sleeves. Work with four strands of CC held together for the sawtooth edging.

+ The gauge swatch was photographed with the wrong side facing.

GAUGE SWATCH

NOTE: The swatch is shown with the WS facing.

With 1 strand of each of MC1 and MC2 held tog, CO 16 sts.

SET-UP ROW: (RS) *Yo, sl 1 pwise with yarn in back (wyb), k1; rep from *—24 sts.

NEXT ROW: *Yo, sl 1 pwise wyb, k2tog (yo and slipped st from previous row); rep from *.

Rep the previous row for both RS and WS rows until piece measures 2¾" (7 cm) from CO, ending with a WS row.

DEC ROW: (RS) *K1, k2tog (yo and slipped st from previous row); rep from *—16 sts rem.

INC ROW: (WS) K1, p2, *M1P (see Glossary), p4; rep from * to last st, M1P, k1—20 sts.

Work basketweave st as foll.

ROW 1: (RS) K5, p5, k5, p4, k1.

ROWS 2–4: Knit the first and last st every row for selvedges, work the other sts as they appear (knit the knits and purl the purls).

ROW 5: (RS) K1, p4, k5, p5, k5.

ROWS 6–8: Work in patt as established.

ROW 9: (RS) Rep Row 1.

Work in rib as established for 3 more rows, ending with a WS row. Change to 4 strands of CC held tog and work sawtooth edging in short-rows as foll.

SHORT-ROW 1: (RS) K1, turn work, k1, turn work.

SHORT-ROW 2: K2, turn, k2, turn.

SHORT-ROW 3: K3, turn, k3, turn.

SHORT-ROW 4: K4, turn, k4, turn.

SHORT-ROW 5: K5, turn, k5, turn.

BO 5 sts—1 st on right needle. Rep Short-rows 2–5 (do not rep Short-row 1) until all sts have been worked. BO last st.

Block as described on page 33.

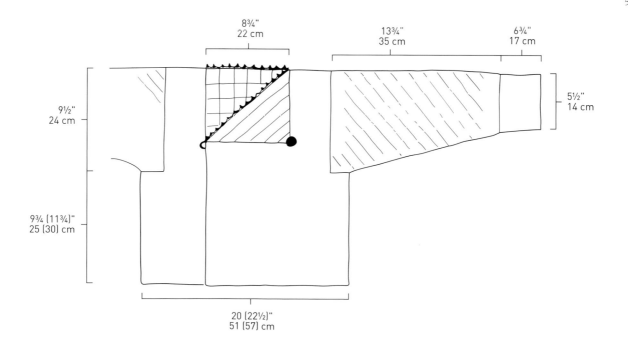

BACK

With one strand each of MC1 and MC2 held tog, CO 80 (90) sts.

SET-UP ROW: (RS) *Yo, sl 1 pwise wyb, k1; rep from *.

NEXT ROW: *Yo, sl 1 pwise wyb, k2tog (yo and slipped st from previous row); rep from *.

Rep the previous row on both RS and WS rows until piece measures 9¾ (11¾)" (25 [30] cm) from CO or desired length to armhole, ending with a WS row.

Shape Armholes

BO 8 sts at beg of next 2 rows as foll: K1, k2tog (yo and slipped st from previous row), slip first st over second st, *k1, slip first st over second st, k2tog, slip first st over second st; rep from * 6 more times, slip st on right-hand needle to left-hand needle, work in patt to end of row—64 (74) sts rem. Work even in patt until armholes measure 2¾" (7 cm), ending with a WS row.

NEXT ROW: Work 14 (20) sts (counting the yo and slipped st as 1 st) in patt, then slip these sts to holder for right back, [k1, k2tog] 17 times, k1, use the backward-loop method (see Glossary) to CO 1 st (for seaming), slip rem 15 (19) unworked sts to holder for left back—36 sts rem.

INC ROW: (WS) K1, p5, *M1P, p4; rep from * 6 more times, p2, use the backward-loop method to CO 1 st (for seaming)—44 sts.

Cont as foll.

ROW 1: (RS) K8, [p7, k7] 2 times, p7, k1.

ROWS 2–10: Knitting the first and last st every row for selvedges, work in patt as established.

ROW 11: (RS) K1, [p7, k7] 3 times, k1.

ROWS 12–20: Knitting the first and last st, work in patt as established.

Rep Rows 1–20 until armholes measure 9½" (24 cm), ending with a WS row. With RS facing, BO all sts in patt.

RIGHT BACK

Slip 14 (20) held right back sts onto needle, ready to work a WS row. Join MC. Using the backward-loop method, CO 1 st (to be used for seaming; knit this st every row), *yo, sl 1 pwise wyb, k2tog; rep from * to end—15 (21) sts. Work in patt as established until brioche section measures same as basketweave section, ending with a WS row. Slip sts onto a holder.

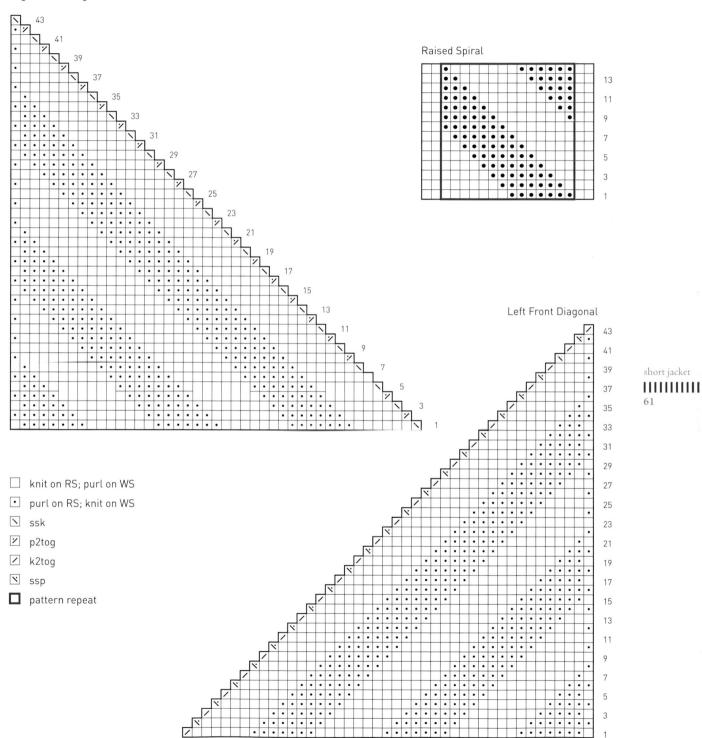

Right Front Diagonal

Raised Spiral

Left Front Diagonal

□ knit on RS; purl on WS

• purl on RS; knit on WS

◼ ssk

◪ p2tog

◩ k2tog

◩ ssp

◼ pattern repeat

LEFT BACK

Slip 15 (19) held left back sts on needle, ready to work a RS row. Join MC. Using the backward-loop method, CO 0 (1) st (to be used for seaming; knit this st every row), then for larger size only M1, then for both sizes, *yo, sl 1 pwise wyb, k2tog; rep from * to end—15 (21) sts. Work in patt as established until brioche section measures same as basketweave section, ending with a WS row. Slip sts onto a holder.

RIGHT FRONT

With MC, CO 56 (62) sts. Work even in brioche st until piece measures same as back to armhole, ending with a RS row.

Shape Armhole

(WS) BO 8 sts at beg of next row as for shaping left back armhole—48 (54) sts rem. Work even in patt until armhole measures 2¾" (7 cm), ending with a WS row.

DEC ROW: (RS) *K1, k2tog; rep from * 16 more times, use the backward-loop method to CO 1 st (seam st; knit every row), slip rem 14 (20) unworked sts to holder—35 sts.
INC ROW: (WS) P3, [M1, p4] 8 times—43 sts. Work Rows 1–43 of Right Front Diagonal chart—1 st rem. Fasten off.

Slip 14 (20) held sts onto working needle, ready to work a RS row. Join MC. Using the backward-loop method, CO 1 st (to be used for seaming; knit this st every row)—15 (21) sts. Work in patt as established until brioche section measures same as basketweave section, ending with a WS row. Place sts on holder.

LEFT FRONT

With MC, CO 56 (62 sts). Work as for right front to beg of armhole shaping, ending with a WS row.

Shape Armhole

(RS) BO 8 sts at beg of next row as for shaping right back armhole—48 (54) sts rem. Work even in patt until armhole measures 2¾" (7 cm), ending with a WS row.

DEC ROW: (RS) Work 14 (20) sts in patt (count the yo and slipped st as 1 st), then slip these sts to a holder, *k1, k2tog; rep from * 16 more times—34 sts rem.
INC ROW: (WS) Using the backward-loop method, CO 1 st, p2, [M1, p4] 8 times—43 sts.

Work Rows 1–43 of Left Front Diagonal chart—1 st rem. Fasten off.

Slip 14 (20) held sts onto working needle, ready to work a WS row. Join MC and cont as for right back. Place sts on holder.

JOIN FRONTS AND BACK AT SHOULDERS

Place 15 (21) held right front shoulder sts on one needle and 15 (21) corresponding right back shoulder sts on another needle. Hold the pieces with RS facing tog and use the three-needle method (see Glossary) to BO the shoulder sts tog. Rep for other shoulder.

With MC threaded on a tapestry needle, use a mattress st (see Glossary) to sew the diagonal patt section to the brioche section of each front. Rep for the back.

SLEEVES

With one strand each of MC1 and MC2 held tog and RS facing, pick up and knit 95 sts evenly spaced around straight edge of armhole opening. Purl 1 WS row. Rep Rows 1–8 of Raised Spiral chart until piece measures 2½" (6.5 cm) from pick-up row, ending with a WS row.

DEC ROW: (RS) K2 (seam st and first St st), k2tog, work in patt to last 4 sts, ssk, k2—2 sts dec'd.

Work 3 rows even in patt. Rep the last 4 rows 18 more times—57 sts rem. Work in patt until sleeve measures 13¾" (35 cm) from pick-up row or 6¾" (15 cm) less than desired total length. On the next row, dec 19 sts evenly spaced—38 sts rem. Work even in brioche st for 6" (15 cm). BO all sts.

FINISHING

Gently steam-press relief patt under a damp cloth, being careful not to flatten the sts. With MC threaded on a tapestry needle, use the mattress st to sew sleeve and side seams.

Neck Edging

With 4 strands of CC held tog, RS facing, and beg at right front neck, pick up (through back loop of edge st only) and knit 45 sts evenly spaced along right front neck edge to shoulder seam, 45 sts across back neck, and 45 sts along left front neck edge—135 sts total. Knit 1 WS row. Work short-rows as foll.

SHORT-ROW 1: (RS) K1, turn work, k1, turn work.
SHORT-ROW 2: K2, turn, k2, turn.
SHORT-ROW 3: K3, turn, k3, turn.
SHORT-ROW 4: K4, turn, k4, turn.
SHORT-ROW 5: K5, turn, k5, turn.

BO 5 sts—1 st on right needle. Rep Short-rows 2–5 (do not rep Short-row 1) until all sts have been worked. BO last st.

Weave in loose ends. Sew large button to WS of right front at corner of diagonal patt and sew small button to RS of left front at corner of diagonal patt.

Button Loop

With MC threaded on a tapestry needle, sew four times back and forth across a ¾" (2 cm) span on left front to form a loop. Work buttonhole sts (see Glossary) around these four strands to stabilize them. Rep for right front.

knit & purl

FINISHED SIZE
Sweater: About 35½ (41¾)" (90 [106] cm) chest circumference. Cap: About 17¾" (45 cm) circumference. Navy sweater shown measures 35½" (90 cm); brown sweater measures 41¾" (106 cm).

YARN
Boy's version: About 200 grams of fingering-weight (#1 Super Fine) yarn. **Man's version:** About 250 grams each of two types of fingering-weight yarn (MC1 and MC2), used held together. **Cap:** About 50 grams each of two types of fingering-weight yarn (MC1 and MC2), used held together.

Shown here: **Boy's version: Highland** (100% wool; 305 yd [279 m]/50 g): denim, 4 skeins.

Man's version and cap: Alpaca 2 (50% merino, 50% alpaca; 270 yd [247 m]/50 g): #011 steel blue (MC1), 5 skeins for sweater, 1 skein for cap. **Highland** (100% wool; 305 yd [279 m]/50 g): tobacco, 5 skeins for sweater, 1 skein for cap.

Knit and Purl, sized for both boys and men, is a good example of how yarn and gauge determine the size and density of a garment. The two sweaters shown here are knitted from the same pattern—with the same number of stitches and rows—but they are different in both size and thickness. The man's version was worked with two strands of the same color throughout, but you could just as easily blend colors as you go. Various shades of blue and green in the same light or dark scale would blend smoothly with each other in the pattern knitting. You could also work with several thin strands held together, changing colors one at a time for gradational stripes.

NEEDLES
Boy's version: Body and sleeves—size U.S. 2 (3 mm): 16" and 32" (40 and 80 cm) circular (cir). Ribbing—size U.S. 1 (2.25 mm): 32" (80 cm) cir and set of 4 or 5 double-pointed (dpn). **Man's version:** Body and sleeves—size U.S. 6 (4 mm): 16" and 32" (40 and 80 cm) circular (cir). Ribbing—size U.S. 5 (3.75 mm): 32" (80 cm) cir and set of 4 or 5 double-pointed (dpn). **Cap:** Size 6 (4 mm): 16" (60 cm) cir and set of 4 or 5 dpn.

Adjust needle size if necessary to obtain the correct gauge.

NOTIONS
Markers (m); stitch holders; tapestry needle.

GAUGE SWATCH

NOTE: The swatch on the left is knitted with one strand each of Alpaca 2 and Highland, used held tog; the swatch on the right is knitted with Highland alone.

With the yarn and larger needles specified for the version of your choice, CO 20 sts. Knit 6 rows, ending with a WS row.

NEXT ROW: (RS) *K2, p2; rep from *. Knitting the first and last st of every row, work rib as established for 4 more rows, ending with a RS row.

Pattern 1
(WS) Knit 1 row, knitting the first and last st of every row, then work 3 rows in St st, ending with a RS row, then knit 1 (WS) row.

Pattern 2
ROW 1: (RS) *K2, p2; rep from * to last 4 sts, k2, p1, k1.
ROW 2: K1, *k2, p2; rep from * to last 3 sts, k3.
ROW 3: K1, p1, *k2, p2; rep from * to last 2 sts, k2.
ROW 4: K1, p2, *k2, p2; rep from * to last st, k1.

Rep 5 rows of Pattern 1.

Pattern 3
ROW 1: (RS) *K4, p4; rep from * to last 4 sts, k4.
ROW 2: K1, p3, *k4, p4; from * to last 4 sts, p3, k1.
ROW 3: Rep Row 1.

Rep 5 rows of Pattern 1.

Pattern 4
ROW 1: (RS) *K2, p2; rep from * to last 4 sts, k2, p1, k1.
ROW 2: K1, p2, *k2, p2; rep from * to last st, k1.
ROW 3: K1, p1, *k2, p2; rep from * to last 2 sts, k2.
ROW 4: K1, *k2, p2; rep from * to last 3 sts, k3.

Rep 5 rows of Pattern 1.

GAUGE

Boy's version: 27 stitches and 43 rows = 4" (10 cm) in charted pattern with Highland on size 2 (3 mm) needles.
Man's version: 23 stitches and 39 rows = 4" (10 cm) in charted pattern with one strand each of Alpaca 2 and Highland yarn, used held together on larger needles. **Cap:** 23 stitches and 39 rows = 4" (10 cm) in charted pattern with one strand each of Alpaca 2 and Highland, used held together, worked in rounds.

NOTES

+ Both sizes are worked with the same number of stitches and rows; the difference is in the yarn and needles.

+ The body and sleeves are worked separately (in the round) to the armholes, then they are joined and the yoke is worked in a single piece to the neck.

+ The front neck is shaped with short-rows (see page 72).

+ The sleeve is 2¼" (5.5 cm) longer than the body on the boy's version and 2½" (6.5 cm) longer than the body on the man's version.

+ When the directions differ for the two versions, directions for the boy's version are given first and directions for the man's version follow in parentheses.

+ The gauge swatch for the man's version is shown in #284 light brown heather (Alpaca 2) and almond green (Highland).

Pattern 5

ROW 1: (RS) *K7, p1; rep from * to last 4 sts, k4.

ROW 2: K1, p2, *k3, p5; rep from * to last st, k1.

ROW 3: K1, p1, *k3, p5; rep from * to last 2 sts, k2.

ROW 4: K1, *k7, p1; rep from * to last 3 sts, k3.

ROW 5: K3, *p1, k7; rep from * to last st, k1.

ROW 6: K2, *p5, k3; rep from * to last 2 sts, p1, k1.

ROW 7: K1, *p5, k3; rep from * to last 3 sts, p2, k1.

ROW 8: K4, *p1, k7; rep from *.

With RS facing, BO all sts knitwise. Block as described on page 33.

BODY

With the yarn and smaller cir needle specified for your version, CO 240 sts. Place marker (pm) and join for working in rnds, being careful not to twist sts. [Purl 1 rnd, knit 1 rnd] 3 times—3 garter ridges. Change to k2, p2 rib and work even for 1½ (2½)" (3.8 [6.5] cm). Change to larger cir needle and work Rnds 1–93 of Body and Sleeves chart (page 70), then work Rnds 1–13 once more—piece measures about 12 (14)" (30.5 [35.5] cm) from CO.

NEXT RND: Keeping in patt working Rnd 14 of chart, work 13 sts and place these sts on a holder, work 120 sts and place the last 13 sts worked onto another holder, work to end—107 sts rem each for front and back; 13 sts on holder for each sleeve. Set aside.

SLEEVES

With smaller dpn, CO 48 sts. Pm and join for working in rnds, being careful not to twist sts. [Purl 1 rnd, knit 1 rnd] 3 times—3 garter ridges. Work in k2, p2 rib until piece measures 1½ (2½)" (3.8 [6.5] cm) from CO. Change to larger dpn and use the M1 method (see Glossary) to inc 8 sts evenly spaced—56 sts. Place another marker after the first st—1 st between markers at underarm. Knit this marked st every rnd. Work Rnds 70–93 of chart (making sure that patts beg and end the same way on side of the marked underarm st), then work Rnds 1–93, then work Rnds 1–14 again and *at the same time* when piece measures 2½ (3½)" (6.5 [9] cm) from CO, inc 1 st each side of marked st as foll.

INC RND: K1, sl m, M1, work in patt to next m, M1, sl m—2 sts inc'd.

Rep inc rnd alternately every 6th and 8th rnd 17 more times, working new sts into patt—92 sts. Work even in patt until sleeve patt ends on same rnd (Rnd 14) as body at underarm, ending 6 sts before marked center st. Place the next 13 sts on holder for underarm removing marker's—79 sts rem. Set aside.

Make another sleeve to match.

YOKE

With larger cir needle and working Rnd 15 of patt, k1 back st, pm, work 105 back sts, pm k1, k1 sleeve st, pm, work 77 sleeve sts, pm, k1, k1 front st, pm, work 105 front sts, pm, k1, k1 sleeve st, pm, work 77 sleeve sts, pm, k1—372 sts total. Work 1 rnd even patt.

DEC RND: *Keeping in patt, work to 2 sts before next m, k2tog, sl m, k2, sl m, k2tog; rep from * 3 more times—8 sts dec'd.

Dec 2 sts at each "seam" in this manner every other row 35 more times and *at the same time* after Rnd 75 of chart has been worked, shape front neck using short-rows as foll.

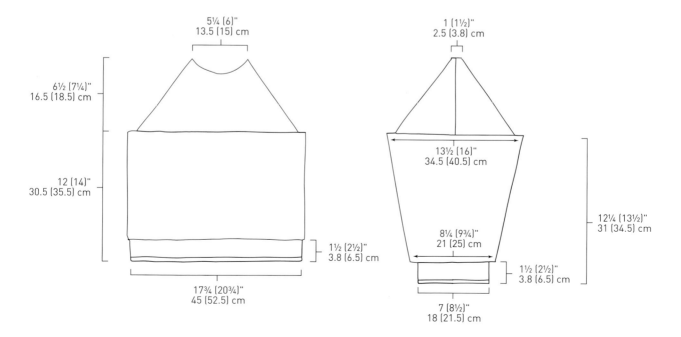

Body and Sleeves

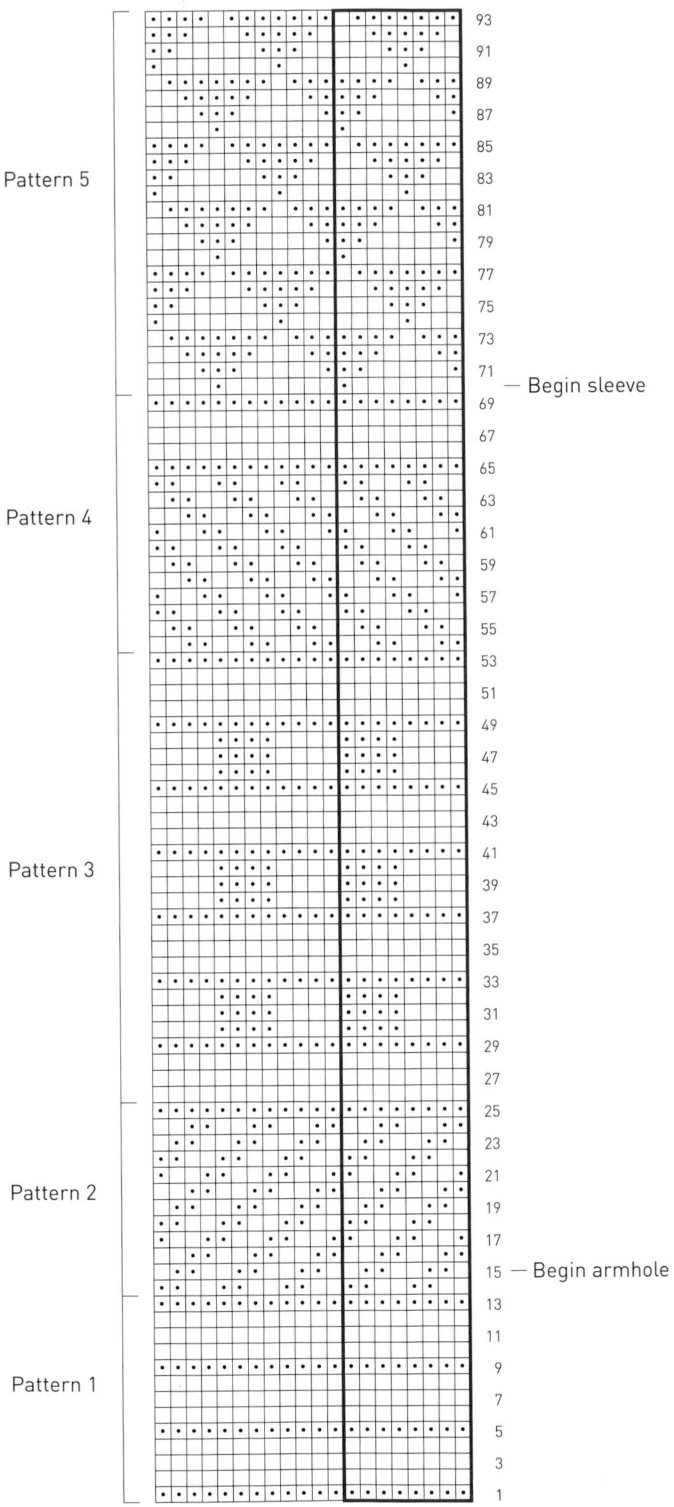

Pattern 5

Pattern 4

Pattern 3

Pattern 2

Pattern 1

— Begin sleeve

— Begin armhole

Cap

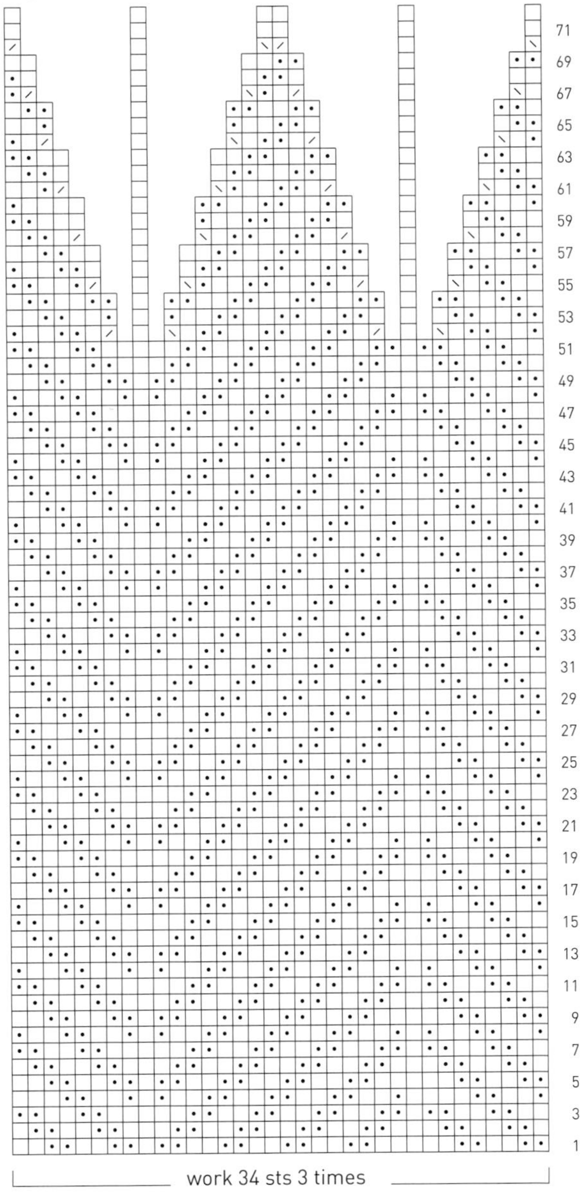

work 34 sts 3 times

☐ knit

• purl

╱ k2tog

╲ ssk

Front Neck

Pm each side of center front 11 sts. Cut yarn and slip all sts to first m to the right-hand needle, turn. Rejoin yarn and beg working short-rows (see page 72) in patt, purling the raglan sts between the markers and working yoke decs as established as foll. (**NOTE:** When working short-rows, always make a yarnover before working back. The yarnover is not counted as a stitch.)

ROW 1: (WS) Yo, work to 4 sts before right front neck m, turn.

ROW 2: (RS) Yo, working as for dec rnd, work to 4 sts before left front neck m, turn.

ROW 3: Yo, work to 2 sts before yo, turn.

Rep Row 3 seven more times, ending with Row 85 of chart—84 sts rem; 35 sts each front and back; 7 sts each sleeve; armhole measures 6½ (7¼)" (16.5 [18.5] cm).

Neckband

With shorter cir needle and RS facing, knit 1 rnd, knitting each yarnover with the following st (the stitch it doesn't lean against) to prevent holes. Work in k2, p2 rib for 1 (2)" (2.5 [5] cm). [Knit 1 rnd, purl 1 rnd] 3 times. BO all sts knitwise.

FINISHING

Place the 13 held sleeve sts on one dpn and 13 corresponding underarm sts on another dpn. Hold the pieces with RS facing tog and use the three-needle method (see Glossary) to BO the sts tog. Weave in loose ends. Block to measurements.

CAP

With size 6 (4 mm) cir needle, CO 102 sts. Place marker (pm) and join for working in rnds, being careful not to twist sts. Pm each side of every 17th st—16 sts bet marked sts. Work Rnds 1–51 of Cap chart, rep the two 34-st sections 3 times around, always knitting the marked sts every other rnd and slipping them on alternate rnds.

DEC RND: (Rnd 52 of chart) * Work in patt to 2 sts before m, ssk or p2tog as necessary to maintain patt, sl m, k1, sl m, k2tog or p2tog as necessary to maintain patt; rep from * 5 more times—12 sts dec'd.

Rep dec rnd every 3rd rnd in this manner 6 more times—18 sts rem, changing to dpn when there are too few sts to fit comfortably on cir needle. Work 2 rnds. On the next rnd, *k2tog; rep from *—9 sts rem. Cut yarn, thread tail through rem sts, pull tight to close hole, and secure to WS. Weave in loose ends.

technique: short-row shaping

||||||||||||||||||||||||||||||||||||||||||||||||||||||||||||||||||||||||||||||||||||||||||||||||||||||||||||||||||

Short-rows allow you to add rows (and therefore length) to a group of stitches on the needles—not all of the stitches are worked all the way across every row. Short-rows are used to create diagonal shapes, such as the sloped shoulders on garments. The key to short-rows is to hide the gap or hole that's created when the worked is turned in the middle of a row.

To work short-rows, work the required number of stitches to the turning point, turn the work around so the other side is facing you, then work back. Either a yarnover or a wrapped stitch is made at the turning point that will be used later to close the gap created at the turning point. Short-rows can begin on either right-side or wrong-side rows.

YARNOVER METHOD
Beginning on a Right-Side Row

With the right-side facing, knit to the turning point, turn the work around so that the wrong side is facing you, make a yarnover on the right needle (Figure 1), then purl to the end. There will now be two more rows of knitting on these stitches (Figure 2). On the next right-side row, knit to the gap, then work the yarnover together with the stitch on the other side of the gap (Figure 3) to close the hole.

Beginning on a Wrong-Side Row

With the wrong-side facing, purl to the turning point, turn the work around so that the right side is facing you, make a yarnover on the right needle (Figure 4), then knit to the end (Figure 5). On the next wrong-side row, purl to the gap, then purl the yarnover together with the next stitch through the back loop (see Glossary; Figure 6).

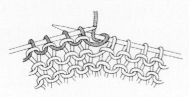

Figure 1

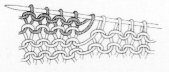

Figure 2

Figure 3

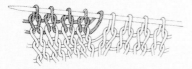

Figure 4

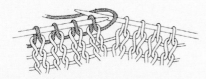

Figure 5

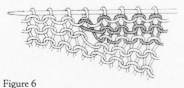

Figure 6

WRAP-AND-TURN METHOD
Right-Side Rows

With right-side facing, knit to the turning point, slip next stitch purlwise (Figure 1), bring the yarn to the front, slip the same stitch back onto the left needle (Figure 2), then turn the work so the purl side is facing and bring the yarn in position for the next stitch—one stitch has been wrapped. When you come to a wrapped stitch on a subsequent row, hide the wrap as follows: Insert right needle tip under the wrap (from the front if wrapped stitch is a knit stitch; from the back if the wrapped stitch is a purl stitch; Figure 3), then into the stitch on the needle, and work the stitch and its wrap together as single stitch.

Wrong-Side Rows

With the wrong-side facing, purl to the turning point, slip the next stitch purlwise to the right needle, bright the yarn to the back of the work (Figure 4), return the slipped stitch onto the left needle, bring the yarn to the front between the needles (Figure 5), and turn the work so that the knit side is facing—one stitch has been wrapped and the yarn is in position for the next stitch. To hide the wrap on a subsequent purl row, work to the wrapped stitch, pick up the wrap with the right needle and place it on the left needle (Figure 6), then purl it together with the wrapped stitch.

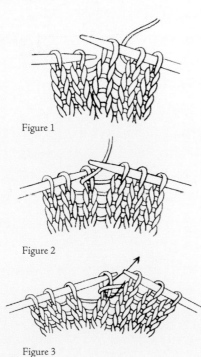

Figure 1

Figure 2

Figure 3

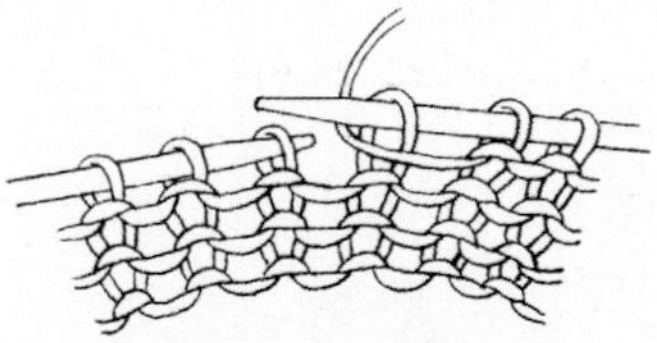

Figure 4

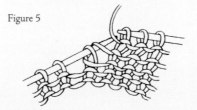

Figure 5

Figure 6

beach flowers

The pattern in this sweater is inspired by the little brightly colored flowers that grow in the cliffs and along the beach where I live. When the wind blows, they make delicate impressions against the sand, which I've tried to capture in this design. To maintain simplicity and order, I worked an embossed diamond motif and embroidered bright stitches at the boundaries between the knit and purl stitches to represent the flowers. In general, textural patterns show up best when worked in light yarns, but if the pattern is simple, it can work just as well with a dark yarn, as shown in the swatch on page 76. If you prefer a less geometric look, embroider the "flowers" randomly across the surface of the knitting.

FINISHED SIZE
About 43¾ (48)" (111 [122] cm) underarm circumference. Sweater shown measures 43¾" (111 cm).

YARN
About 250 grams of a main color (MC1) of fingering-weight (#1 Super Fine) yarn and 250 grams of a main color (MC2) of laceweight (#0 Lace) yarn, used held together.

Shown here: **Alpaca 2** (50% merino, 50% alpaca; 270 yd [247 m]/50 g): #100 natural or #011 steel blue (MC1), 5 (5) skeins. **Wool 1** (100% wool; 340 yd [311 m]/50 g): #2s light gray heather or #4s charcoal heather (MC2), 5 (5) skeins.

NEEDLES
Size U.S. 4 (3.5 mm): 16" and 24" (40 and 60 cm) circular (cir); spare needle for three-needle bind-off. Adjust needle size if necessary to obtain the correct gauge.

NOTIONS
Marker (m); stitch holders; tapestry needle; small amounts of your choice of Alpaca 2 or Isager 1 in bright colors for embroidery (CC).

GAUGE
22 stitches and 28 rows = 4" (10 cm) in charted Diamond pattern with one strand each of MC1 and MC2 held together.

NOTES
+ Work with one strand each of MC1 and MC2 held together throughout.
+ Work the embroidery with two strands of your choice of CC held together. (Many of the colors shown here have been discontinued.)

GAUGE SWATCH

With one strand each of MC1 and MC2 held tog, CO 26 sts. Knit 5 rows.

NEXT ROW: (RS) K2, *p3, k3; rep from *.
NEXT ROW: K1, p2, *k3, p3; rep from * to last 5 sts, k3, p1, k1.

Work in rib patt as established for 3 more rows. Knitting the first and last st of every row for selvedge sts and beg and ending as indicated for body, work Rows 1–12 of Diamond chart (page 79) 2 times. BO all sts.

Block swatch as described on page 33. With two strands of contrasting yarn threaded on a tapestry needle, embroider star stitches (see illustration on page 79) in colors as desired at boundaries between diamonds.

BODY
Welts

With one strand each of MC1 and MC2 held tog and longer cir needle, CO 123 (135) sts. Do not join. Working back and forth in rows, knit 5 rows.

NEXT ROW: (RS) K3, *k3, p3; rep from * to last 6 sts, k6.
NEXT ROW: (WS) *K3, p3; rep from * to last 3 sts, k3.

Rep the last 2 rows until piece measures 2¾" (7 cm) from CO, ending with a WS row. Place sts on holder. Make another piece to match but leave sts on needle.

Join Welts

With RS facing, place 123 (135) held welt sts onto same cir needle as 123 (135) live welt sts—246 (270) sts total. Work across all sts in rib patt and *at the same time* work [k2tog] 2 times at beg of each welt and [k2tog] 1 time at end of each welt—240 (264) sts rem. Place marker (pm) and join for working in rnds, being careful not to twist sts. Rep Rows 1–12 of Diamond chart until piece measures 11¾ (13¾)" (30 [35] cm) from CO.

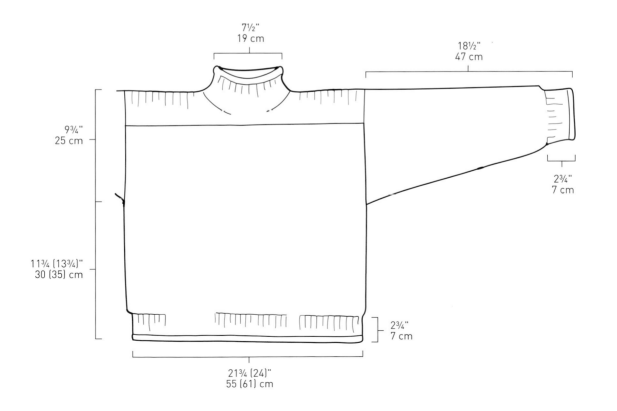

DIVIDE FOR FRONT AND BACK

Knit into the front and back of the first st (k1f&b), work 119 (131) sts in patt for back, turn work—121 (133) sts for back; rem 120 (132) sts will be worked later for front.

Back

Knitting the first and last st of every row for selvedge sts, work 121 (133) back sts in patt until armholes measure 7" (18 cm), ending with a WS row.

NEXT ROW: (RS) Knit into the front, back, and front of the next st (k1f&b&f), k1, p3, *k3, p3; rep from * to last 2 sts, k1f&b&f, k1—125 (137) sts.
NEXT ROW: (WS) K1, p3, *k3, p3; rep from * to last st, k1.

Knitting the first and last st of every row for selvedge sts, work in k3, p3 rib as established until armhole measures 9¾" (25 cm). Place sts on a holder.

Front

Rejoin yarn to 120 (132) held front sts with RS facing, k1f&b, work in patt to end—121 (133) sts. Work as for back until armhole measures 7¼" (18.5 cm), ending with a WS row—125 (137) sts.

Shape Neck

With RS facing, work 56 (61) sts, place center 13 (15) sts on a holder for front neck, join new yarn and work to end—56 (61) sts rem each side. Working each side separately, at each neck edge, BO 4 sts 2 times, then BO 2 sts 4 (5) times—40 (43) sts rem for each shoulder. Place sts on holders.

SLEEVES

With one strand each of MC1 and MC2 held tog and shorter cir needle, CO 51 sts. Do not join. Working back and forth in rows, knit 5 rows.

NEXT ROW: (RS) K3, *p3, k3; rep from *.

Knitting the first and last st of every row for selvedge sts, work in rib as established until piece measures 2¾" (7 cm) from CO, ending with a WS row. Rep Rows 1–12 of Diamond chart and *at the same time* inc 1 st each end of needle inside selvedge sts every 4th row 29 times, working new sts into patt—109 sts. Work even until piece measures about 18½" (47 cm) from CO, ending with Row 6 or 12 of chart. BO all sts.

FINISHING

Block pieces to measurements. Weave in loose ends.

Join Front and Back at Shoulders

Place 40 (43) held right front shoulder sts on one needle. Hold the front and back pieces with RS facing tog and use the three-needle method (see Glossary) to BO the 40 (43) shoulder sts tog. Place the next 45 (51) sts from back on a holder for back neck. Rep for three-needle bind-off for 40 (43) sts of other shoulder.

Diamond

•														•	
							•								11
•						•	•	•					•		
					•	•		•	•						9
•				•	•		•		•	•			•		
			•	•		•		•		•	•				7
•		•	•		•		•		•		•	•		•	
			•	•		•		•		•	•				5
•				•	•		•		•	•			•		
					•	•		•	•						3
•						•	•	•					•		
							•								1

☐ knit on RS; purl on WS

• purl on RS; knit on WS

◻ pattern repeat

Note: When working in rounds, only work the 12-stitch pattern repeat; when working in rows, work the stitches outside the pattern repeat box as well.

STAR STITCH

To make the base of the star, bring threaded needle out from back to front at lower left edge of the intended star, then insert it at the upper right edge, back out at the lower right edge, and in again at the upper left edge. Taking smaller stitches, make a cross on top of the previous stitches.

Neckband

With one strand each of MC1 and MC2 held tog, shorter cir needle, and RS facing, pick up and knit 45 (51) sts evenly spaced around front neck opening, then knit 45 (51) sts from back neck holder, maintaining k3, p3 rib as much as possible across front and back neck—90 (102) sts total. Work in rib as established until neckband measures about 4" (10 cm) or desired length. [Purl 1 rnd, knit 1 rnd] 2 times, then purl 1 rnd—3 garter ridges. BO all sts.

With yarn threaded on a tapestry needle, use the mattress st (see Glossary) to sew sleeve tops into armholes. Sew sleeve seams. Steam-press seams.

Embroidery

With two strands of contrasting yarn in desired color threaded on a tapestry needle, work star sts (see at right) at boundaries between diamonds.

pearls

Pearls combines seed-stitch and slip-stitch patterns, some of the most dependable ones in my knitting repertoire. Each has a lovely structure that works well in many types of garments and, at the same time, is easy to knit. Seed stitch is actually a type of displaced ribbing. I've also chosen displaced chain stitch (the first two sts at the center front edge are slipped but kept in the ribbing as they are slipped by working the first stitch in stockinette with the yarn kept on the wrong side while it's slipped and the second stitch in reverse stockinette with the yarn kept on the right side while it's slipped) as an edging.

FINISHED SIZE
About 41¾ (45¼)" (106 [115] cm) bust circumference, buttoned. Sweater shown measures 41¾" (106 cm).

YARN
About 250 (300) grams of a main color (MC1) of laceweight (#0 Lace) yarn and about 200 (250) grams of a main color (MC2) of a different laceweight yarn. About 50 grams of a contrast color (CC1) of laceweight yarn and about 50 grams of a contrast color (CC2) of a sportweight (#1 Super Fine) yarn.

Shown here: **Alpaca 1** (100% alpaca; 437 yd [400 m]/50 g): #500 black (MC1), 5 (6) skeins. **Wool 1** (100% wool; 340 yd [311 m]/50 g): #101 dark blue (MC2), 4 (5) skeins; #28s coral (CC1) 1 (1) skein. **Alpaca 2** (50% merino, 50% alpaca; 270 yd [247 m]/50 g): #014 orange (CC2), 1 (1) skein.

NEEDLES
Size U.S. 6 (4 mm): straight and 32" (60 cm) circular (cir). Adjust needle size if necessary to obtain the correct gauge.

NOTIONS
Stitch holders; tapestry needle; removable markers; seven ¾" (2 cm) buttons.

GAUGE
18 stitches and 31 rows = 4" (10 cm) in seed stitch with two strands each of MC1 and MC2 held together.

NOTE
+ Work with two strands each of MC1 and MC2 (for a total of four strands) held together for the main color; work with two strands of CC1 and one strand of CC2 for the contrast color.

+ The fronts are worked from the shoulders down to the lower edge, then stitches for the back are picked up along the cast-on row and the back is worked downward in a similar way.

GAUGE SWATCH

With two strands each of MC1 and MC2 held tog, CO 23 sts.

ROW 1: (WS) Sl 1 purlwise (pwise) with yarn in front (wyf; edge st), sl 1 pwise with yarn in back (wyb), *p1, k1; rep from * to last st, k1.

ROW 2: (RS) Sl 1 pwise wyf, *k1, p1; rep from * to last 8 sts, k1, [k1, p1] 3 times, k1.

Rep these 2 rows until piece measures 2¼" (5.5 cm) from CO, ending 7 sts before end of last rep of Row 2, place last 7 sts on holder unworked—16 sts rem.

INC ROW: (WS) K2, *M1 (see Glossary), k2; rep from * to end—23 sts.

Join 2 strands of CC1 and 1 strand of CC2 held tog (designated CC from here on) and work 23 live sts in slip-stitch patt as foll.

ROW 1: (RS) With CC, *k1, sl 1 pwise wyb; rep from * to last st, k1.

ROW 2: With CC, *k1, sl 1 wyf; rep from * to last st, k1.

ROWS 3 AND 4: With one strand each of MC1 and MC2 held tog (2 strands total), knit.

ROW 5: With CC1, k1, *k1, sl 1 wyb; rep from *, to last 2 sts, k2.

ROW 6: With CC1, k1, *k1, sl 1 wyf; rep from * to last st, k1.

ROWS 7 AND 8: With one strand each of MC1 and MC2 held tog, knit.

Rep Rows 1–8 three more times. Cut yarn and set aside.

Place the 7 held sts onto needle and join 2 strands each of MC1 and MC2 (4 strands total) with RS facing. On the next row (RS), M1, [k1, p1] 3 times, k1—8 sts. Knitting the new st every row, work in rib as established until piece is as long as slip-st section, ending with a RS row.

DEC ROW: (WS) Work 7 sts in rib as established, place 23 held slip-st sts on empty needle, k2tog (last st of ribbing with first st of slip-st section), *p1, k2tog; rep from * to last st, p1—23 sts rem.

NEXT ROW: (RS) *P1, k1; rep from * to last 7 sts, [k1, p1] 3 times, k1.

With WS facing, BO all sts. With yarn threaded on a tapestry needle, use the mattress st (see Glossary) to sew the ribbing to the slip-st section.

Block as described on page 33.

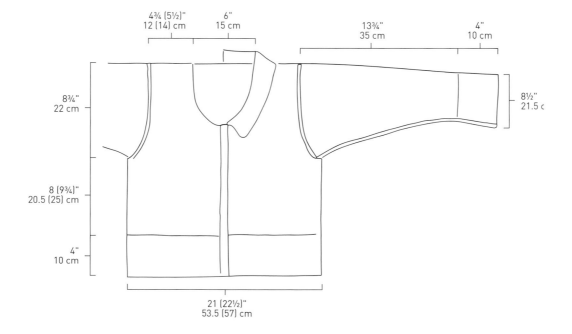

RIGHT FRONT

With 2 strands each of MC1 and MC2 held tog (4 strands total) and straight needles, CO 21 (25) sts.

ROW 1: (WS) *K1, p1; rep from * to last st, k1.
ROW 2: (RS) K2, p1, k1, *k1, p1; rep from * to last st, k1.

Rep Rows 1 and 2 until piece measures 3½" (9 cm) from CO, ending with a WS row.

Shape Neck

ROW 1: (RS; inc row) Keeping in patt, work to last st, M1 (see Glossary), k1—1 st inc'd.
ROW 2: K2, *p1, k1; rep from * to end.
ROW 3: (inc row) Keeping in patt, work to last st, M1, k1—1 st inc'd.
ROW 4: *K1, p1; rep from * to last st, k1.
ROWS 5–12: Rep Rows 1–4 two more times—27 (31) sts.
ROWS 13 AND 15: (RS) Work in patt as established, then use the backward-loop method (see Glossary) to CO 2 sts at the end of the row—2 sts inc'd; 31 (35) sts after Row 15.

ROWS 14 AND 16: *K1, p1; rep from * to last st, k1.
ROW 17: Keeping in patt, work to end of row, then use the backward-loop method to CO 7 sts for front band—38 (42) sts total.
ROW 18: (WS) Sl 1 purlwise (pwise) with yarn in front (wyf; edge st), sl 1 pwise with yarn in back (wyb), *p1, k1; rep from * to end.
ROW 19: K2, p1, k1, *k1, p1; rep from * to last 8 sts, k1, [k1, p1] 3 times, k1.

Rep the last 2 rows until piece meas ½" (1.3 cm) from 7 CO sts, ending with a WS row.

BUTTONHOLE ROW 1: (RS) Work in patt to last 7 sts: k1, [k2tog] 2 times, work to end of row.
BUTTONHOLE ROW 2: (WS) Sl 1 pwise wyf, sl 1 wyb, p1, using the backward-loop method to CO 2 sts, work to end as for Row 18—piece measures about 6" (16 cm) from CO.

SHAPE ARMHOLE

Cont working buttonhole rows every 2" (5 cm) until 7 buttonholes have been completed and *at the same time* shape armhole as foll.

ROW 1: (RS; inc row) K2, p1, k1, M1, *k1, p1; rep from * to last 8 sts, k1, [k1, p1] 3 times, k1—1 st inc'd.

ROW 2: (WS) Sl 1 wyf, sl 1 wyb, *p1, k1; rep from * to last 5 sts, p2, k1, p1, k1.

ROW 3: (inc row) K2, p1, k1, M1, *p1, k1; rep from * to last 7 sts, [k1, p1] 3 times, k1—1 st inc'd.

ROW 4: Sl 1 wyf, sl 1 wyb, *p1, k1; rep from * to end.

Rep Rows 1–4 four more times—48 (52) sts; armholes measure about 8¾" (22 cm). Place sts on holder.

LEFT FRONT

With two strands each of MC1 and MC2 held tog (4 strands total) and straight needles, CO 21 (25) sts.

ROW 1: (WS) *K1, p1; rep from * to last st, k1.

ROW 2: (RS) *K1, p1; rep from * to last 5 sts, k2, p1, k2.

Rep Rows 1 and 2 until piece measures 3½" (9 cm) from CO, ending with a WS row.

Shape Neck

ROW 1: (RS; inc row) K1, M1, work to end in patt—1 st inc'd.

ROW 2: *K1, p1; rep from * to last 2 sts, k2.

ROW 3: (inc row) K1, M1, work to end in patt—1 st inc'd.

ROW 4: *K1, p1; rep from * to last st, k1.

ROWS 5–11: Rep Rows 1–4 once, then rep Rows 1–3 once more—27 (31) sts.

ROWS 12 AND 14: (WS) Rep Row 4, then use the backward-loop method to CO 2 sts at the end of the row—2 sts inc'd; 31 (35) sts after Row 14.

ROWS 13 AND 15: (RS) *K1, p1; rep from * to last 5 sts, k2, p1, k2.

ROW 16: (WS) Keeping in patt, work to end of row, then use the backward-loop method to CO 7 sts for front band—38 (42) sts.

ROW 17: Sl 1 pwise wyf (edge st), sl 1 pwise wyb, [k1, p1] 2 times, k1, *k1, p1; rep from * to last 5 sts, k2, p1, k2.

ROW 18: *K1, p1; rep from * to end.

Rep the last 2 rows until piece measures 6¼" (16 cm) from CO, ending with a WS row.

Shape Armhole

ROW 1: (RS; inc row) Sl 1 pwise wyb, sl 1 pwise wyf, [k1, p1] 2 times, k1, *k1, p1; rep from * to last 5 sts, k1, M1, k1, p1, k2—1 st inc'd.

ROW 2: (WS) [K1, p1] 2 times, *p1, k1; rep from * to last st, p1.

ROW 3: (inc row) Sl 1 pwise wyb, sl 1 pwise wyf, [k1, p1] 2 times, k1, *k1, p1; rep from * to last 4 sts, M1, k1, p1, k2—1 st inc'd.

ROW 4: (WS) *K1, p1; rep from * to end.

Rep Rows 1–4 four more times—48 (52) sts; armhole measures about 8¾" (22 cm). Place sts on holder.

BACK

With two strands each of MC1 and MC2 (4 strands total), straight needles, and RS facing, pick up and knit 21 (25) sts into back loops of left shoulder CO edge, use the backward-loop method to CO 27 sts, then pick up and knit 21 (25) sts into back loops of right shoulder CO edge—69 (77) sts total.

ROW 1: (WS) *K1, p1; rep from * to last st, k1.

ROW 2: (RS) K2, p1, k1, *k1, p1; rep from * to last 5 sts, k2, p1, k2.

Rep Rows 1 and 2 until piece measures 6¼" (16 cm) from pick-up row.

Shape Armholes

ROW 1: (RS; inc row) K2, p1, k1, M1, *k1, p1; rep from * to last 5 sts, k1, M1, k1, p1, k2—2 sts inc'd.

ROW 2: [K1, p1] 2 times, *p1, k1; rep from * to last 5 sts, p2, k1, p1, k1.

ROW 3: (inc row) K2, p1, k1, M1, *p1, k1; rep from * to last 5 sts, p1, M1, k1, p1, k2—2 sts inc'd.

ROW 4: *K1, p1; rep from * to last st, k1.

Rep Rows 1–4 four more times—89 (97) sts.

JOIN FRONTS AND BACK

Cont working buttonhole rows on right front every 2" (5 cm) until there are 7 completed buttonholes, join fronts and back as foll.

JOINING ROW: With RS facing, cir needle, and keeping in patt, work across 48 (52) left front sts from holder, use the backward-loop method to CO 5 sts for left underarm, work 89 (97) back sts, use the backward-loop method to CO 5 sts for right underarm, then work 48 (52) right front sts—195 (211) sts total.

ROW 1: (WS) Sl 1 pwise wyf, sl 1 pwise wyb, *k1, p1; rep from * to last st, k1.

ROW 2: (RS) Sl 1 pwise wyb, sl 1 pwise wyf, [k1, p1] 2 times, k1, *k1, p1; rep from * to last 8 sts, k1, [k1, p1] 3 times, k1.

Rep Rows 1 and 2 until piece measures 8 (9¾)" (20.5 [25] cm) from joining row, or about 4" (10 cm) less than desired total length, ending 7 sts before the end of last rep of Row 2, place last 7 sts on holder unworked—188 (204) sts rem.

Edging

(WS; inc row) K4, *M1, k2; rep from * to last 8 sts, k1; place last 7 sts on holder unworked for front band—269 (293) sts on needle; 7 sts on each of two holders. Join CC (two strands of CC1 and one strand of CC2) and work 269 (293) sts in slip-st patt as for gauge swatch: Work Rows 1–8 five times, then work Rows 1–4 once. Set aside.

Place the 7 held right front band sts onto straight needle and with WS facing, join two strands each of MC1 and

MC2. With RS facing, M1, [k1, p1] 3 times, k1—8 sts. Knitting the new st every row and working buttonholes as established, work in rib until piece is as long as slip-st section, ending with a WS row. Place these sts onto holder. Place the 7 held left front band sts onto straight needle and with WS facing, join two strands each of MC1 and MC2 held tog. With WS facing, M1, [p1, k1] 3 times, p1—8 sts. Cont as for right front band, omitting buttonholes and ending with a WS row.

DEC ROW: (RS) With cir needle, work 7 front sts in rib as established, p2tog (last st of ribbing with first st of slip-st section), k1, *p1, k1; rep from * to last 9 sts, p2tog (last st of slip-st section with first st of other front ribbing), work to end in rib as established—283 (307) sts rem.

Work 1 (WS) row even in rib as established. With RS facing, BO all sts in patt as foll: K1, *k2tog, slip the previous st over the 2 sts worked tog; rep from * to end. With yarn threaded on a tapestry needle, use the mattress st (see Glossary) to sew the ribbing to the slip-st section.

SLEEVES

Measure down and mark 6" (15 cm) from each shoulder on front and back. With two strands each of MC1 and MC2 (4 strands total), straight needles, and RS facing, pick up and knit 60 sts evenly spaced between markers. Working back and forth in rows, work in seed st and *at the same time* use the backward-loop method to CO 5 sts at the end of pick-up row, then at the end of each of the next 5 rows, ending with a WS row—90 sts. Use the backward-loop method to CO 2 sts at the end of the next 2 rows, ending with a WS row—94 sts.

ROWS 1 AND 3: (RS) K2, work in seed st as established to last 2 sts, k2.

ROWS 2 AND 4: K1, p1, work in seed st as established to last 2 sts, p1, k1.

DEC ROW: (RS) K2, ssk, work in seed st as established to last 4 sts, k2tog, k2—2 sts dec'd.

Dec 1 st each end of needle in this manner every 4th row 21 more times—50 sts rem. Work even in patt until piece measures 13¾" (35 cm) from pick-up row or about 4" (10 cm) less than desired total length, ending with a RS row. Use the backward-loop method to CO 1 st—51 sts.

INC ROW: (WS) K1, p1, M1, p1, *k2, M1; rep from * to last 2 sts, p1, M1, p1, use the backward-loop method to CO 1 st—77 sts.

Place the first 4 and the last 4 sts onto separate holders; leave the 2 strands of each MC attached—69 sts on needle; 4 sts on each of two holders. Join CC and work 69 sts in slip-st patt as for gauge swatch: work Rows 1–8 five times, then work Rows 1–4 once. Place these sts onto a holder.

With RS facing, place the 4 held sts at the beg of the row onto straight needles and cont working with 2 strands each of MC1 and MC2, k2, p1, k1, M1—5 sts. Knitting the new st every row, work in rib as established until piece is as long as slip-st section, ending with a WS row. Place these sts onto holder. With RS facing, place the 4 held sts at the end of the row onto straight needles and join 2 strands each of MC1 and MC2, M1, [p1, k1] 2 times—5 sts. Cont as for sts from beg of RS row until piece is as long as slip-st section, ending with a WS row.

DEC ROW: (RS) With cir needle, k2, p1, k1, p2tog (last st of ribbing with first st of slip-st section), k1, *p1, k1; rep from * to last 6 sts, p2tog (last st of slip-st section with first st of left front ribbing), k1, p1—77 sts rem.

Work 1 (WS) row in rib as established. With RS facing, BO all sts in patt as foll: K1, *k2tog, slip the previous st over the 2 sts worked tog; rep from * to end. With yarn threaded on a tapestry needle, use the mattress st to sew the ribbing to the slip-st section.

FINISHING

Sew the edges of the sleeve cuffs to the slip-st sections as for the gauge swatch. Weave in loose ends. Block to measurements.

Collar

With two strands each of MC1 and MC2, cir needle, RS facing, and beg on right front neck edge on buttonhole band, pick up and knit 8 sts across buttonhole band, 36 sts to shoulder seam, 31 sts across the back neck, 36 sts to buttonband, then 8 sts across buttonband—119 sts total.

ROW 1: (WS) *K1, p1; rep from * to last st, k1.
ROW 2: (RS) BO 7 sts in rib, work to last 8 sts in seed st, [k1, p1] 3 times, k2—112 sts rem.
ROW 3: BO 7 sts in rib, work to last st in seed st, k1—105 sts rem.

Slipping the first st and knitting the last st of every row for edge sts, work even in patt until piece measures 2" (5 cm) from pick-up row, ending with a WS row.

DEC ROW: (RS) Sl 1 pwise wyb, k2tog, work to last 3 sts, ssk, k1—2 sts dec'd.

Cont to dec 2 sts every other row 5 more times—93 sts rem. BO all sts.

Carefully steam-press collar, being careful not to flatten it. Sew buttons to left front opposite buttonholes.

march

I find it exciting to experiment with various colors in the triangles. The slip-stitch pattern consists of a background color or a network in very thin yarn that is worked in garter stitch. The color fields, which I call "buds," are worked with thicker yarn. They are also worked in garter stitch, but every other stitch is slipped with yarn behind when worked on the right side and with yarn in front from the wrong side. For added texture, thick and thin yarns alternate every two rows.

FINISHED SIZE
About 48¼" (122.5 cm) chest circumference.

YARN
Shown here: **Alpaca 2** (50% merino, 50% alpaca; 270 yd [247 m]/50 g): #500 black (MC1), 4 skeins; #011 steel blue (CC1), #012 grayed olive (CC2), #019 light blue (CC3), #017 antique gold (CC4), #020 teal (CC5), and #2105 light gray heather (CC6), 1 skein each (used double). **Wool 1** (100% wool; 340 yd [311 m]/50 g): #47 steel gray (MC2) and #2s light gray heather (MC3), 2 skeins each.

NEEDLES
Size U.S. 2 (3 mm): straight. Adjust needle size if necessary to obtain the correct gauge.

NOTIONS
Removable markers; stitch holders; tapestry needle; 5" (12.5 cm) non-separating zipper; sharp-point sewing needle; contrasting sewing thread for basting zipper; matching thread for sewing zipper.

GAUGE
30 stitches and 54 rows = 4" (10 cm) in slip-stitch pattern.

NOTES
+ Work with two strands of the contrasting colors held together.
+ Knit the first and last stitch of every row for a knotted edge stitch.
+ Always slip stitches purlwise, holding the yarn in back on right-side rows and in front on wrong-side rows.
+ Work the color blocks in the intarsia method of twisting the yarns around each other on the wrong side at color changes (see page 49).

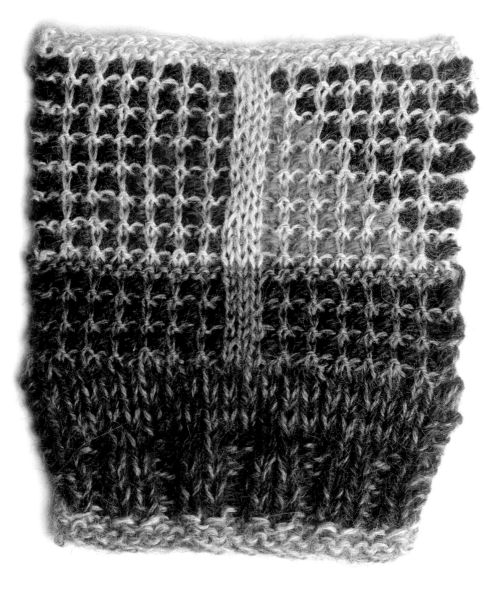

GAUGE SWATCH

The swatch is worked with MC2, then MC3, as the background and MC1 as the slip-stitch "buds."

With two strands of MC3 held tog, CO 22 sts. Knit 3 rows. Cut off MC3. Join MC1 and MC2. Cont with one strand each of MC1 and MC2 held tog and work in k2, p2 rib until piece measures ¾" (2 cm) from CO. Work in St st (knit RS rows; purl WS rows) for ¾" (2 cm), ending with a WS row. Cut off MC1.

INC ROW: (RS) With MC2 alone, k3, *M1 (see Glossary), k2; rep from * to last st, k1—31 sts.

NEXT ROW: (WS) K14, p3, k14.

Beg with a RS row and knitting the first and last st of every row, alternate 2 rows of slip-st "buds" as foll.

ROW 1: (RS) With MC1, k1, [k1, sl 1 (see Notes)] 6 times, k1, sl the center 3 sts, [k1, sl 1] 6 times, k2.

ROW 2: Rep Row 1, holding yarn in front while slipping sts (see Notes).

ROW 3: With MC2, knit.

ROW 4: With MC2, k14, p3, k14.

ROWS 5–12: Rep Rows 1–4 two more times. Cut off MC2.

ROWS 13 AND 14: With MC3, rep Rows 3 and 4.

Cut off MC1, leaving a 60" (152.5 cm) tail. With a single strand of MC1 as the background and two 60" (152.5 cm) strands of desired contrast color (CC1, CC2, CC3, CC4, or CC5), work as foll.

ROW 15: Rep Row 1, working the first st with MC1, then work with two strands of the desired CC to the center 3 sts, sl these 3 sts, then work with two strands of a second CC to the last st, work last st with the other two strands of MC1.

ROW 16: Rep Row 2, working with the same colors used for Row 15 and twist the yarns around each other at color changes in the intarsia method (see page 49) to avoid holes.

ROW 17: With MC2, knit.

ROW 18: With MC2, k15, p3, k15.

Cont as charted, rep Rows 15–18 and working 1 less "bud" in CC with each Row 15 until no contrasting sts rem, ending with 2 rows of MC2. BO all sts.

Block as described on page 33.

Slip-Stitch Pattern

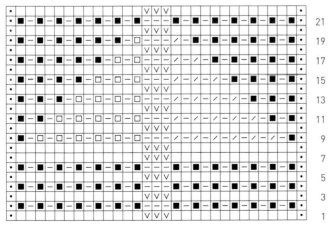

Note: Each square on the chart represents one stitch and two rows (a RS row followed by a WS row).

Gauge Swatch

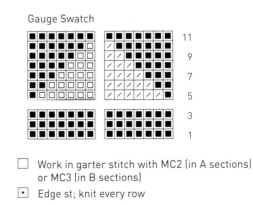

☐ Work in garter stitch with MC2 (in A sections) or MC3 (in B sections)

· Edge st; knit every row

− Sl 1 pwise wyb on RS; sl 1 pwise wyf on WS

V Knit on RS, purl on WS with MC2 or MC3

■ Contrast color of your choice (shown in MC1)

▣ Contrast color of your choice (shown in #014 Orange)

▨ Contrast color of your choice (shown in CC4)

Right Front

Left Front

B

A

B

A

B

A

Back Neck

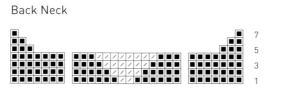

7
5
3
1

■ CC1 (steel blue)
◩ MC1 (black)
◢ CC2 (grayed olive)
⬝ CC5 (teal)
◺ CC3 (light blue)
⊠ CC6 (light gray heather)
▢ CC4 (antique gold)

FRONT

With two strands of MC3 held tog, CO 120 sts. Knit 3 rows, ending with a WS row. Cut off both yarns. Join one strand each of MC1 and MC2 and work in k2, p2 rib for 2¼" (5.5 cm). Work in St st (knit RS rows; purl WS rows) for ¾" (2 cm), ending with a WS row. On the next row (RS), with MC2 alone, knit and *at the same time* inc 61 sts evenly spaced—181 sts. With MC2, purl 1 (WS) row. Working colors as shown on the chart at left, work as foll.

ROW 1: (RS) With colors indicated on chart, k1, [k1, sl 1 (see Notes)] 6 times, k1, sl 3, *[k1, sl 1] 13 times, k1, sl 3; rep from * to last 14 sts, [k1, sl 1] 6 times, k2.

ROW 2: Rep Row 1, holding yarn in front while slipping sts (see Notes).

ROW 3: With MC2, knit.

ROW 4: With MC2, k14, p3, *k27, p3; rep from * to last 14 sts, k14.

Rep Rows 1–4 for each row shown on chart until one full rep of A is completed. With MC3, work Rows 3 and 4, then rep Rows 1–4 with MC3 instead of MC2 until one full rep of B is completed. With MC2, work Rows 3 and 4, then rep Rows 1–4 until half of a rep of A is completed, ending with Row 2—piece measures about 13¾" (35 cm) from CO.

Shape Armholes

Keeping in patt, BO 13 sts at beg of next 2 rows—155 sts rem.

ROW 1: (RS) With colors indicated on chart, k1, sl 3 sts, *[k1, sl 1] 13 times, k1 sl 3 sts; rep from * to last st, k1.

ROW 2: Rep Row 1, holding yarn in front while slipping sts.

ROW 3: With MC2, knit.

ROW 4: With MC2, k1, p3, *k27, p3; rep from * to last st, k1.

Rep Rows 1–4 for each row shown on chart until the other half of A is completed. With MC3, work Rows 3 and 4, then rep Rows 1–4 with MC3 instead of MC2 until one full rep of B is completed. With MC2, work Rows 3 and 4—armholes measure about 6½" (16.5 cm).

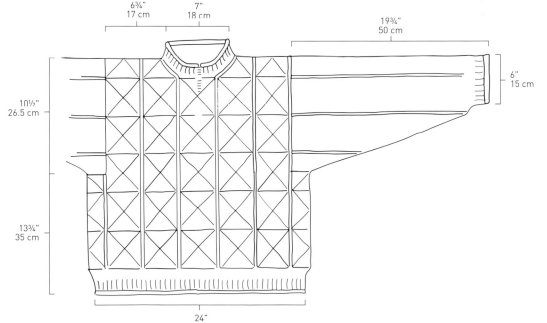

Back

Divide for Placket

Working Row 1 of patt as established above, work 77 sts, join new yarns and BO center st, work to end—77 sts rem each side. Work each side separately, keeping the 3 sts to each side of the divide in MC1 as foll.

ROW 1: (WS) With colors indicated on chart, k1, sl 3, *[k1, sl 1] 13 times, k1, sl 3; rep from * to 13 sts before divide, [k1, sl 1] 5 times, with MC1 k3; on other side, with MC1 k3, then with colors indicated, [sl 1, k1] 5 times, *sl 3, [k1, sl 1] 13 times, k1; rep from * to last 4 sts, sl 3, k1.

ROW 2: With MC2, knit to 3 sts before divide, sl 3; on other side, sl 3, knit to end.

ROW 3: With MC2, k1, p3, *k27, p3; rep from * to 13 sts before divide, k10, sl 3; on other side, sl 3, k10, *p3, k27; rep from * to last 4 sts, p3, k1.

ROW 4: (RS) With colors indicated, k1, sl 3, *[k1, sl 1] 13 times, k1, sl 3; rep from * to 13 sts before divide, [k1, sl 1] 5 times, with MC1 k3; on other side, with MC1 k3, with colors indicated, [sl 1, k1] 5 times, *sl 3, [k1, sl 1] 13 times, k1; rep from * to last 4 sts, sl 3, k1.

Rep Rows 1–4 until one full rep of A is completed ending with Row 3. With MC3, work Rows 2 and 3—slit measures 4¼" (11 cm).

Shape Neck

At each neck edge, place 12 sts on holders—65 sts rem each side. Cut off yarn on right front.

ROW 1: (RS) With colors indicated, k1, sl 3, [k1, sl 1] 13 times, k1, sl 3, [k1, sl 1] to 7 sts before divide, k1, k2tog, sl 3, k1; on other side, rejoin yarn (on first rep of this row only), k1, sl 3, ssk, [k1, sl 1] to 1 st before next set of 3 slipped sts, k1, sl 3, [k1, sl 1] 13 times, k1, sl 3, k1—2 sts dec'd (1 st at each neck edge).

ROW 2: With colors indicated, k1, sl 3, [k1, sl 1] 13 times, k1, sl 3, [k1, sl 1] to 6 sts before divide, k2, sl 3, k1; on other side k1, sl 3, k1, [k1, sl 1] to 1 st before next set of 3 slipped sts, k1, sl 3, [k1, sl 1] 13 times, k1, sl 3, k1.

ROW 3: With MC2, knit to 6 sts before divide, k2tog, k4; on other side, k4, ssk, knit to end—2 sts dec'd (1 st at each neck edge).

ROW 4: With MC2, k1, p3, k27, p3, knit to 4 sts before divide, p3, k1; on other side, k1, p3, knit to next set of 3 slipped sts, p3, knit to last 4 sts, p3, k1.

Rep Rows 1–4 six more times—51 sts rem each side. Place sts on holders.

BACK

CO and work as for front but use MC1 and MC2 throughout.

ROW 1: (RS) With MC 1, k1, [k1, sl 1] 6 times, k1, sl 3, *[k1, sl 1] 13 times, k1, sl 3; rep from * to last 14 sts, [k1, sl 1] 6 times, k2.

ROW 2: Rep Row 1, holding yarn in front while slipping sts.

ROW 3: With MC2, knit.

ROW 4: With MC2, k14, p3, *k27, p3; rep from * to last 14 sts, k14.

Rep Rows 1–4 until piece measures about 13¾" (35 cm) from CO.

Shape Armholes

Keeping in patt, BO 13 sts at beg of next 2 rows—155 sts rem.

Rep Rows 1–4 as for front armholes until armholes measure about 10½" (26.5 cm).

Place markers each side of center 59 sts, rep Rows 1–4 as for front armholes 4 times and *at the same time* work sts between markers in colors indicated on Back Neck chart on page 92, ending after Row 4.

Shape Neck

Keeping in patt, work 54 sts, place the next 47 sts on a holder, join new yarn and work to end—54 sts each side. Working each side separately, at each neck edge dec 1 st just inside the outermost MC2 st every RS row 3 times—51 sts rem each side.

Back Detail

JOIN FRONT AND BACK

Place 51 held right front shoulder sts on one needle and 51 corresponding right back shoulder sts on another needle. Hold the pieces with RS facing tog and use the three-needle method (see Glossary) to BO the sts tog. Rep for other shoulder.

SLEEVES

With two strands of MC3 held tog, CO 56 sts. Knit 3 rows, ending with a WS row. Cut off MC3. Join one strand each of MC1 and MC2 held tog and work in k2, p2 rib for 2¼" (5.5 cm). Work in St st for ¾" (2 cm), ending with a WS row. On the next row (RS), with MC2 alone, inc 33 sts evenly spaced—89 sts. Purl 1 (WS) row. Mark the center 27 sts. **NOTE:** Increases are introduced at the same time as the pattern is set up; read all the way through the foll section before proceeding.

ROW 1: (RS) With MC1, k1, [k1, sl 1] 13 times to 4 sts before m, k1, sl 3, sl m, [k1, sl 1] 13 times, k1, sl m, sl 3, [k1, sl 1] 13 times to last 2 sts, k2.

ROW 2: Rep Row 1, holding the yarn in front while slipping sts.

ROW 3: With MC2, knit.

ROW 4: With MC2, k14, p3, *k27, p3; rep from * to last 14 sts, k14.

At the same time beg with Row 1, then alternating every 4th and 6th row for a total of 46 times, inc 1 st inside each selvedge st as foll.

INC ROW: (RS) K1, M1, work as established to last st, M1, k1—2 sts inc'd.

Work inc'd sts into the slipped st patt as they appear, maintaining 27 sts between each set of 3 slipped sts—181 sts. Work even in patt until piece measures 19¾" (50 cm) from CO. Mark each end of last row for armhole placement. Work even in patt for 2" (5 cm) more. BO all sts.

FINISHING

Weave in loose ends. Block to measurements. With yarn threaded on a tapestry needle, use the mattress st (see Glossary) to sew tops of sleeves into armholes. Sew sleeve and side seams.

Neckband

Slip 12 neck sts from right front holder to working needle preparing to work a RS row. With MC1, k3 sts along neck, then with one strand each of MC1 and MC2 held tog, k9, then pick up and knit 15 sts along front neck to shoulder, k50 back neck sts, pick up and knit 15 sts along other front neck to held sts, k9 held left front sts, then with MC1, k3—104 sts total. Knitting the first 3 and last 3 sts with MC1 throughout, purl 1 WS row.

NEXT ROW: (RS) K3 with MC1, change to MC1 and MC2 held tog and work k2, *p2, k2; rep from * to last 3 sts, k3 with MC1 alone.

Work 7 more rows in patt as established or until front opening measures same length as zipper. With two strands of MC3 held tog, knit 6 rows, ending with a WS row.

Facing

Cont in St st with one strand of the contrasting color of your choice until piece is as long as the ribbed section, ending with a WS row.

NEXT ROW: (RS) Work 27 sts, join new yarn and BO 50 sts across back neck, work to end—27 sts rem each side.

Working each side separately, cont in St st and use the backward-loop method (see Glossary) to CO 10 sts at each shoulder edge at end of previous row and the next WS row for facing.

SHIFT ROW: (RS) K1, k2tog, work to 1 st before neck edge, M1, k1; on other side, k1, M1, work to last 3 sts, ssk, k1.

Work 1 WS row even. Rep the last 2 rows 24 more times. Work even until the St st section measures 1¼" (3.2 cm) longer than front placket. BO all sts.

Zipper

Sew zipper in place (see Glossary). With yarn threaded on a tapestry needle, sew neck facing to WS.

Steam-press seams under a damp cloth, being careful not to flatten the knitting.

zigzag top

This summer top is worked in one of my favorite techniques of combining increases and decreases to form a chevron or zigzag pattern. The neck and armhole shaping are created automatically by the pattern stitch. Because this top is worked from the top down, you can easily make small adjustments to the sizing, such as making the body narrower by casting on fewer stitches for the underarm or making the lower body wider by omitting decreases after the armhole.

FINISHED SIZE
About 38¾ (42½, 47½)" (98.5 [108, 120.5] cm) bust circumference. Top shown measures 38¾" (98.5 cm).

YARN
About 200 (250, 300) grams of a main color (MC1) of fingering-weight (#1 Super Fine) yarn and about 200 (250, 300) grams of a main color (MC2) of another fingering-weight yarn, used held together.

Shown here: **Viscolin** (50% viscose, 50% linen; 202 yd [185 m]/50 g): #40 chartreuse or #100 natural (MC1), 4 (5, 6) skeins. **Bomuld** (100% cotton; 228 yd [208 m]/50 g): #15 grass green or #0 natural (MC2), 4 (5, 6) skeins.

NEEDLES
Body—size U.S. 4 (3.5 mm): 24" (60 cm) circular (cir). Edging—size U.S. 3 (3.25 mm): 24" (60 cm) cir. Adjust needle size if necessary to obtain the correct gauge.

NOTIONS
Stitch holders; markers (m) in assorted colors; tapestry needle.

GAUGE
26 stitches and 27 rows = 4" (10 cm) in pattern stitch on larger needle with one strand each of MC1 and MC2 held together.

NOTES
+ Work with one strand each of MC1 and MC2 held together throughout.

+ Slip the first stitch of every row purlwise (pwise) with yarn in back (wyb) on RS rows and with yarn in front (wyf) on WS rows.

+ The gauge swatch can be used as the garter-stitch diamond that begins the shoulder for size small.

+ To widen the top below the armholes, increase in Rnd 10 as follows: *Knit to next m, M1, sl m, k1, M1, knit to next m, sl m; rep from * 8 more times—16 sts inc'd.

+ To work the body straight from the armhole, omit the decreases in Rnd 10.

+ The gauge swatch shown on page 100 was worked in colors that have been discontinued.

GAUGE SWATCH

With one strand each of MC1 and MC2 held tog and larger needle, CO 12 sts. Slipping the first st of every row (see Notes), knit 24 rows.

SET-UP ROW: (RS) Sl 1 pwise wyb, k10, knit into the front and back of the next st (k1f&b), pick up and knit 12 sts in the back loops of the chain edge sts along the selvedge edge—25 sts total.

ROW 1: (WS) Sl 1 pwise wyf, p23, k1.

ROW 2: (RS) Sl 1 pwise wyb, k2tog, k9, M1 (see Glossary), k1, M1, k9, ssk, k1.

ROWS 3–8: Rep Rows 1 and 2 three times.

ROW 9: (WS) Sl 1 pwise wyf, k24.

ROW 10: Rep Row 2.

ROWS 11–20: Rep Rows 1–10 once.

ROW 21: (RS) Sl 1 pwise wyb, k2tog, k9, M1, k1, M1, k9, ssk, k1.

ROW 22: Sl 1 pwise wyf, k24.

Rep the last 2 rows once more. BO all sts. Block as described on page 33.

FRONT

Shoulder Straps

With one strand each of MC1 and MC2 held tog and larger needle, CO 12 (15, 19) sts. Working back and forth in rows and slipping the first st of every row (see Notes), knit 24 (30, 38) rows.

SET-UP ROW: (RS) Sl 1 pwise wyb, k10 (13, 17), knit into the front and back of the next st (k1f&b), pick up and knit 12 (15, 19) sts in the back loops of the chain edge sts along the selvedge edge—25 (31, 39) sts total.

ROW 1: (WS) Sl 1 pwise wyf, p23 (29, 37), k1.

ROW 2: (RS) Sl 1 pwise wyb, k2tog, k9 (12, 16), M1 (see Glossary), k1, M1, k9 (12, 16), ssk, k1.

ROWS 3–8: Rep the last 2 rows 3 more times.

ROW 9: (WS) Sl 1 pwise wyf, k24 (30, 38).

ROW 10: Rep Row 2.

Rep Rows 1–9 once more. Place sts on a holder. Make another piece to match but leave the sts on the needle.

Shape Front Neck

(RS) Sl 1 pwise wyb, k2tog, k9 (12, 16), M1, k1, M1, k9 (12, 16), ssk, k1 across strap sts, use the backward-loop method (see Glossary) to CO 49 sts, k1, k2tog, k9 (12, 16), M1, k1, M1, k9 (12, 16), ssk, k1 across sts of other strap—99 (111, 127) sts total.

ROW 1: (WS) Sl 1 purlwise wyf, purl to last st, k1.

ROW 2: (RS) Sl 1 pwise wyb, k2tog, k9 (12, 16), M1, k1, M1, k9 (12, 16), ssk, k1, k2tog, k22, M1, k1, M1, k22, ssk, k1, k2tog, k9 (12, 16), M1, k1, M1, k9 (12, 16) ssk, k1.

ROWS 3–8: Rep Rows 1 and 2 three times.

ROW 9: (WS) Sl 1 pwise wyf, knit to end.

ROW 10: Rep Row 2.

Rep Rows 1–9 once more. Place sts onto a holder; set aside.

BACK

With one strand each of MC1 and MC2 held tog and RS facing, pick up and knit 12 (15, 19) sts along CO edge of left shoulder diamond, pick up and knit 1 st at corner, then pick up and knit 12 (15, 19) more sts along the final edge of the diamond; use the backward-loop method to CO 49 sts, then pick up and knit 25 (31, 39) sts along right shoulder strap as before—99 (111, 127) sts total. Work back and forth in patt as for front, working Rows 1–10 of neck shaping three times, then work Rows 1–9 once more.

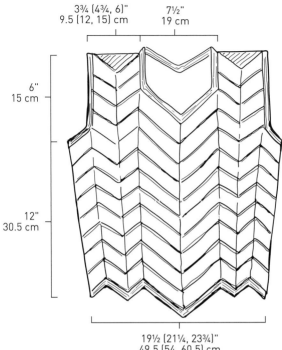

3¾ (4¾, 6)"
9.5 (12, 15) cm

7½"
19 cm

6"
15 cm

12"
30.5 cm

19½ (21¼, 23¾)"
49.5 (54, 60.5) cm

JOIN FRONT AND BACK

(RS; Row 10 of patt) Keeping in patt, work 99 (111, 127) back sts, use the backward-loop method to CO 27 sts for underarm, work 99 (111, 127) front sts, CO 27 sts for other underarm—252 (276, 308) sts total. Pm and join for working in rnds.

RND 1: Knit.

RND 2: Place different colored markers while working around as foll: *K1, k2tog, k9 (12, 16), M1, place marker (pm), k1, M1, k9 (12, 16), ssk, pm, k1, k2tog, k22, M1, pm, k1 (center back/front st), M1, k22, ssk, pm, k1, k2tog, k9 (12, 16), M1, pm, k1, M1, k9 (12, 16), ssk, pm, k1, k2tog, k11, M1, pm, k1 (center underarm st), M1, k11, ssk, pm; rep from * once more.

RNDS 3–8: Rep Rnds 1 and 2 three times, slipping markers.

RND 9: Purl.

RND 10: (Dec rnd) *K1, k2tog, knit to next m, sl m, knit to 2 sts before next m, ssk, sl m; rep from * 7 more times—16 sts dec'd.

Rep Rnds 1–10 three more times, knitting the first st after each marker and working the inc or dec on each side of the knit st as established—172 (196, 228) sts rem. [Work Rnds 1–9, then work Rnd 2] 4 times—piece measures about 18" (45.5 cm) from CO, or desired length. Purl 1 rnd. Rep Rnd 2. Rep the last 2 rnds 2 more times. BO all sts.

FINISHING

Weave in loose ends. Block to measurements.

Neckband

With smaller cir needle, RS facing, and beg at left shoulder seam, pick up and knit 18 sts to neck edge, 24 sts along front neck to center st, pm, pick up 25 sts to left strap, 18 sts along left strap, 24 sts along back neck to center st, pm, pick up 25 sts to right strap—134 sts. Pm and join for working in rnds.

RND 1: Purl.

RND 2: *Knit to 2 sts before m, ssk, sl m, k1, k2tog; rep from * once more, knit to end—4 sts dec'd.

Rep these 2 rnds 2 more times—122 sts rem. BO all sts purlwise.

Armbands

With smaller cir needle, RS facing, and beg at center underarm st, pick up and knit 101 sts evenly spaced around armhole edge. [Purl 1 rnd, knit 1 rnd] 3 times. BO all sts purlwise.

zigzag jacket

This zippered jacket combines chevron zigzags with intarsia color blocks and four-stitch cables. The jacket begins with a solid square at the shoulder, then the body is worked downward to the hem, with waist decreases hidden in the pattern stripes along the way. The sleeves are worked downward from the underarms, making it easy to adjust the total length for a custom fit.

FINISHED SIZE
About 37¼ (40½, 43¾)" (94.5 [103, 111] cm) bust circumference, zipped. Jacket shown measures 40½" (103 cm).

YARN
About 100 (150, 200) grams of one color (A1) and 50 grams each of three colors (B1, C1, and D1) of laceweight (#0 Lace) yarn. About 150 (200, 250) grams of one color (A2) and 50 grams each of three colors (B2, C2, and D2) of fingering-weight (#1 Super Fine) yarn.

Shown here: **Alpaca 1** (100% alpaca; 437 yd [400 m]/50 g): #020 teal (A1), 2 (3, 4) skeins; #016 chartreuse (B1), #019 light blue (C1), and #013 dusty plum (D1), 1 skein each. **Highland** (100% wool; 305 yd [279 m]/50 g): crocus (A2), 3 (4, 5) skeins; almond green (B2), topaz (C2), and sweet pea (D2), 1 skein each.

NEEDLES
Body and sleeves—size U.S. 2 (3.0 mm): straight, 16" (40 cm), and 24" (60 cm) circular (cir). Neckband—size U.S. 1 (2.5 mm): 24" (60 cm) cir. Adjust needle sizes if necessary to obtain the correct gauge.

NOTIONS
Cable needle (cn); markers (m); tapestry needle; 16 (16, 18)" (40.5 [40.5, 45.5] cm) separating zipper to match finished length of front opening.

GAUGE
30 stitches and 28 rows = 4" (10 cm) in zigzag pattern on larger needles with one strand each of A1 and A2 held together; 25 stitches and 36 rows = 4" (10 cm) in stockinette stitch on larger needles with one strand each of A1 and A2 held together.

GAUGE SWATCH

With one strand each of A1 and A2 held tog (referred to as A) and larger needles, CO 15 sts. Slipping the first st purlwise (pwise) with yarn in front (wyf) for edge st, knit 30 rows—15 garter ridges; piece forms a square.

SET-UP ROW: (RS) Sl 1 pwise wyf (edge st), sl 1 pwise with yarn in back (wyb), k15, pick up and knit 15 sts (1 st in each edge st) along the selvedge edge of the square—30 sts.

NEXT ROW: (WS) Sl 1 pwise wyf (edge st), sl 1 pwise wyf, purl to last st, k1.

Work in patt as foll.

ROW 1: (RS) Sl 1 pwise wyf, sl 1 pwise wyb, k2tog, k9, yo, k4, yo, k9, ssk, k2.

ROW 2: (WS) Sl 1 pwise wyf, sl 1 pwise wyf, p27, k1.

ROW 3: (cable row) Sl 1 pwise wyf, sl 1 pwise wyb, k2tog, k9, yo, sl next 2 sts on cn and hold in front of work, k2, k2 from cn, yo, k9, ssk, k2.

ROW 4: Rep Row 2.

Rep Rows 1–4 two more times, then work Rows 1–3 once more. Cont in patt as foll.

ROWS 4, 6, AND 12: (WS; color change) With one strand each of C1 and C2 held tog (referred to as C), sl 1 pwise wyf, sl 1 pwise wyf, p13, change to one strand each of D1 and D2 held tog (referred to as D), p14, k1.

ROWS 5, 13, AND 15: Sl 1 pwise wyf, sl 1 pwise wyb, k2tog, k9, yo, k2, change to C, k2, yo, k9, ssk, k2.

ROW 7: (cable and color change) Sl 1 pwise wyf, sl 1 pwise wyb, k2tog, k9, yo, sl next 2 sts onto cn and hold in front of work, k2 with C, k2 from cn with D, change to C, yo, k9, ssk, k2.

ROWS 8 AND 10: Sl 1 pwise wyf, sl 1 pwise wyf, p11, p2 with D, p2 with C, change to D, p12, k1.

ROW 9: Sl 1 pwise wyf, sl 1 pwise wyb, k2tog, k9, yo, k2 with C, k2 with D, change to C, yo, k9, ssk, k2.

NOTES

+ Work with one strand each of A1 and A2 for "A," one strand each of B1 and B2 for "B," one strand each of C1 and C2 for "C," and one strand each of D1 and D2 for "D."

+ Use the intarsia method (see page 49) of twisting the yarns around each other on the wrong side of the knitting at color changes to prevent holes.

+ The sweater begins with garter-stitch squares at the shoulders and is worked downward to the hem.

+ The gauge swatch can be used as the garter-stitch diamond that begins the shoulder for size medium.

+ The sweater shown on the model on page 104 was worked in different colors than the sample garment shown photographed flat. The instructions match this sample garment.

ROW 11: (cable and color change) Sl 1 pwise wyf, sl 1 pwise wyb, k2tog, k9, yo, sl next 2 sts onto cn and hold in front, k2 with D, k2 from cn with C, yo, k9, ssk, k2.

ROWS 14 AND 16: Sl 1 pwise wyf, sl 1 pwise wyf, k11, p2, change to D, p2, k11, p1, k1.

ROW 17: Sl 1 pwise wyf, sl 1 pwise wyb, k2tog, k9, yo, k2, change to C, k2, yo, k9, ssk, k2.

ROW 18: Rep Row 14.

With RS facing, BO all sts, maintaining colors as established. Block as described on page 33.

RIGHT FRONT

With one strand each of A1 and A2 held tog (A) and larger straight needles, CO 13 (15, 17) sts. Slipping the first st of every row pwise wyf (edge st), knit 26 (30, 34) rows.

SET-UP ROW: (RS) Sl 1 pwise wyf, k13 (15, 17), pick up and knit 13 (15, 17) sts through the back loops of the chain edge sts along the selvedge edge—26 (30, 34) sts total.

Cont as foll.

ROWS 1 AND 3: (WS) K1 (edge st), purl to last st, k1 (edge st).

ROW 2: (RS) K1, k2tog, k8 (10, 12), yo, k4, yo, k8 (10, 12), ssk, k1.

ROW 4: K1, k2tog, k8 (10, 12), yo, sl next 2 sts onto cn and hold in front of work, k2, k2 from cn, yo, k8 (10, 12), ssk, k1.

Rep Rows 1–4 three more times, using the backward-loop method (see Glossary) to CO 27 sts for neck at end of last row—4 cable turns; 53 (57, 61) sts. Cont as foll.

ROWS 1 AND 3: (WS) Sl 2 pwise wyf, purl to last st, k1.

ROW 2: (RS) K1, k2tog, k8 (10, 12), yo, k4, yo, k8 (10, 12), ssk, k2, k2tog, k22, M1 (see Glossary), k2.

ROW 4: K1, k2tog, k8 (k10, 12), yo, sl next 2 sts onto cn and hold in front, k2, k2 from cn, yo, k8 (10, 12), ssk, k2, k2tog, k22, M1, k2.

Rep Rows 1–4 four (five, six) more times, then work Rows 1–3 once more—piece measures 5½ (6¼, 6¾)" (14 [16, 17] cm) from pick-up row—9 (10, 11) cable turns total. Place sts on a holder.

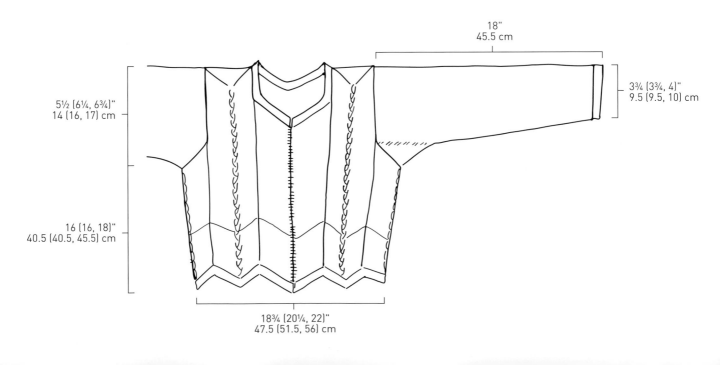

18"
45.5 cm

3¾ (3¾, 4)"
9.5 (9.5, 10) cm

5½ (6¼, 6¾)"
14 (16, 17) cm

16 (16, 18)"
40.5 (40.5, 45.5) cm

18¾ (20¼, 22)"
47.5 (51.5, 56) cm

LEFT FRONT

CO and work as for right front until 4 cable turns are completed.

ROW 1: K1, purl to end, then use the backward-loop method to CO 27 sts for neck—53 (57, 61) sts total. Work all subsequent reps of Row 1 as for Row 3 (do not CO more sts).

ROW 2: (RS) Sl 1 pwise wyf, sl 1 pwise wyb, M1, k22, ssk, k2, k2tog, k8 (10, 12), yo, k4, yo, k8 (10, 12), ssk, k1.

ROW 3: K1 (edge st), purl to last st, k1 (edge st).

ROW 4: Sl 1 pwise wyf, sl 1 pwise wyb, M1, k22, ssk, k2, k2tog, k8 (10, 12), yo, sl next 2 sts onto cn and hold in front, k2, k2 from cn, yo, k8 (10, 12), ssk, k1.

Rep Rows 1–4 four (five, six) more times, then work Rows 1–3 once more—piece measures 5½ (6¼, 6¾)" (14 [16, 17] cm) from pick up row—9 (10, 11) cable turns total. Place sts on a holder.

BACK

With A, RS facing, and larger straight needles, pick up and knit 13 (15, 17) sts along the CO edge of left front, then 13 (15, 17) sts through back loops of the chain edge sts along the selvedge edge, use the backward-loop method to CO 54 new sts, then pick up and knit 13 (15, 17) sts along the CO edge of right front, then 13 (15, 17) sts through back loops of the chain edge sts along the selvedge edge—106 (114, 122) sts total.

ROWS 1 AND 3: (WS) K1 (edge st), purl to last st, k1 (edge st).

ROW 2: (RS) K1, k2tog, k8 (10, 12), yo, k4, yo, k8 (10, 12), ssk, k2, k2tog, k22, yo, k4, yo, k22, ssk, k2, k2tog, k8 (10, 12), yo, k4, yo, k8 (10, 12), ssk, k1.

ROW 4: K1, k2tog, k8 (10, 12), yo, sl next 2 sts onto cn and hold in front, k2, k2 from cn, yo, k8 (10, 12), ssk, k2, k2tog, k22, yo, sl next 2 sts onto cn and hold in front, k2, k2 from cn, yo, k22, ssk, k2, k2tog, k8 (10, 12), yo, sl next 2 sts onto cn and hold in front, k2, k2 from cn, yo, k8 (10, 12), ssk, k1.

Rep Rows 1–4 eight (nine, ten) more times, then work Rows 1–3 once more—piece measures 5½ (6¼, 6¾)" (14 [16, 17] cm) from pick-up row—9 (10, 11) cable turns total. Place sts on holder.

JOIN FRONTS AND BACK

(RS; Row 4 of patt) With larger 24" (60 cm) cir needle and keeping in patt, work 53 (57, 61) held left front sts, place marker (pm), use the backward-loop method to CO 34 (38, 42) sts for underarm, pm, work 106 (114, 122) back sts, pm, use the backward-loop method to CO 34 (38, 42) sts for other underarm, pm, work 53 (57, 61) held right front sts—280 (304, 328) sts total. Slipping markers (sl m) every row, work back and forth in rows as foll.

ROWS 1 AND 3: (WS) Sl 2 pwise wyf, purl to last st, k1 (edge st).

ROW 2: (RS; Row 2 of patt) Work 53 (57, 61) sts of left front, sl m, k1, k2tog, k12 (14, 16), yo, k4, yo, k12 (14, 16), ssk, k1, sl m, work 106 (114, 122) sts of back, sl m, k1, k2tog, k12 (14, 16), yo, k4, yo, k12 (14, 16), ssk, k1, sl m, work 53 (57, 61) sts of right front.

ROW 4: Work 53 (57, 61) sts of left front, sl m, k1, k2tog, k12 (14, 16), yo, sl next 2 sts onto cn and hold in front, k2, k2 from cn, yo, k12 (14, 16), ssk, k1, sl m, work 106 (114, 122) sts of back, sl m, k1, k2tog, k12 (14, 16), yo, sl next 2 sts onto cn and hold in front, k2, k2 from cn, yo, k12 (14, 16), ssk, k1, sl m, work 53 (57, 61) sts of right front.

Rep Rows 1–4 ten more times—piece measures 6¼" (16 cm) from underarm CO—21 (22, 23) cable turns total.

Before proceeding, wind 16 yarn butterflies (6 with C; 5 each with B and D).

ROWS 1 AND 3: (color change) (WS) With C, sl 2 pwise wyf, p25, change to B, p13 (15, 17), change to D, p13 (15, 17), sl m, change to C, p17 (19, 21), change to B, p17 (19, 21), sl m, change to D, p13 (15, 17), change to C, p13 (15, 17), change to B, p27, change to D, p27, change to C, p13 (15, 17), change to B, p13 (15, 17), sl m, change to D, p17 (19, 21), change to C, p17 (19, 21), sl m, change to B, p13 (15, 17), change to D, p13 (15, 17), change to C, p27.

ROW 2: Sl 1 pwise wyf, sl 1 pwise wyb, M1, k22, ssk, k1, change to D, k1, k2tog, k8 (10, 12), yo, k2, change to B, k2, yo, k8 (10, 12), ssk, k1, sl m, change to C, k1, k2tog, k12 (14, 16), yo, k2, change to D, k2, yo, k12 (14, 16), ssk, k1, sl m, change to B, k1, k2tog, k8 (10, 12), yo, k2, change to C, k2, yo, k8 (10, 12), ssk, k1, change to D, k1, k2tog, k22, yo, k2, change to B, k2, yo, k22, ssk, k1, change to C, k1, k2tog, k8 (10, 12), yo, k2, change to D, k2, yo, k8 (10, 12), ssk, k1, sl m, change to B, k1, k2tog, k12 (14, 16), yo, k2, change to C, k2, yo, k12 (14, 16), ssk, k1, sl m, change to D, k1, k2tog, k8 (10, 12), yo, k2, change to B, k2, yo, k8 (10, 12), ssk, k1, change to C, k1, k2tog, k22, M1, k2.

ROW 4: (cable row) Sl 1 pwise wyf, sl 1 pwise wyb, M1, k22, ssk, k1, change to D, k1, k2tog, k8 (10, 12), yo, sl next 2 sts onto cn and hold in front, k2 with B, k2 from cn with D, change to B, yo, k8 (10, 12), ssk, k1, sl m, change to C, k1, k2tog, k12 (14, 16), yo, sl next 2 sts onto cn and hold in front, k2 with D, k2 from cn with C, change to D, yo, k12 (14, 16), ssk, k1, sl m, change to B, k1, k2tog, k8 (10, 12), yo, sl next 2 sts onto cn and hold in front, k2 with C, k2 from cn with B, change to C, yo, k8 (10, 12), ssk, k1, change to D, k1, k2tog, k22, yo, sl next 2 sts onto cn and hold in front, k2 with B, k2 from cn with D, change to B, yo, k22, ssk, k1, change to C, k1, k2tog, k8 (10, 12), yo, sl next 2 sts onto cn and hold in front, k2 with D, k2 from cn with C, change to D, yo, k8 (10, 12), ssk, k1, sl m, change to B, k1, k2tog, k12 (14, 16), yo, sl next 2 sts onto cn and hold in front, k2 with C, k2 from cn with B, change to C, yo, k12 (14, 16), ssk, k1, sl m, change to D, k1, k2tog, k8 (10, 12), yo, sl next 2 sts onto cn and hold in front, k2 with B, k2 from cn with D, change to B, yo, k8 (10, 12), ssk, k1, change to C, k1, k2tog, k22, M1, k2.

ROWS 5 AND 7: Sl 2 pwise wyf, purl to last st in colors as they appear, k1.

ROW 6: Sl 1 pwise wyf, sl 1 pwise wyb, M1, k22, ssk, k1, change to D, k1, k2tog, k8 (10, 12), yo, k2 with B, k2 with D, change to B, yo, k8 (10, 12), ssk, k1, sl m, change to C, k1, k2tog, k12 (14, 16), yo, k2 with D, k2 with C, change to D, yo, k12 (14, 16), ssk, k1, sl m, change to B, k1, k2tog, k8 (10, 12), yo, k2 with C, k2 with B, change to C, yo, k8 (10, 12), ssk, k1, change to D, k1, k2tog, k22, yo, k2 with B, k2 with D, change to B, yo, k22, ssk, k1, change to C, k1, k2tog, k8 (10, 12), yo, k2 with D, k2 with C, change to D, yo, k8 (10, 12), ssk, k1, sl m, change to B, k1, k2tog, k12 (14, 16), yo, k2 with C, k2 with B, change to C, yo, k12 (14, 16), ssk, k1, sl m, change to D, k1, k2tog, k8 (10, 12), yo, k2 with B, k2 with D, change to B, yo, k8 (10, 12), ssk, k1, change to C, k1, k2tog, k22, M1, k2.

ROW 8: (cable row) Sl 1 pwise wyf, sl 1 pwise wyb, M1, k22, ssk, k1, change to D, k1, k2tog, k8 (10, 12), yo, sl next 2 sts onto cn and hold in front, k2 with D, change to B, k2 from cn, yo, k8 (10, 12), ssk, k1, sl m, change to C, k1, k2tog, k12 (14, 16), yo, sl next 2 sts onto cn and hold in front, k2 with C, change to D, k2 from cn, yo, k12 (14, 16), ssk, k1, sl m, change to B, k1, k2tog, k8 (10, 12), yo, sl next 2 sts onto cn and hold in front of work, k2 with B, change to C, k2 from cn, yo, k8 (10, 12), ssk, k1, change to D, k1, k2tog, k22, yo, sl next 2 sts onto cn and hold in front, k2 with D, change to B, k2 from cn, yo, k22, ssk, k1, change to C, k1, k2tog, k8 (10, 12), yo, sl next 2 sts onto cn and hold in front, k2 with C, change to D, k2 from cn, yo, k8 (10, 12), ssk, k1, sl m, change to B, k1, k2tog, k12 (14, 16), yo, sl next 2 sts onto cn and hold in front of work, k2 with B, change to C, k2 from cn, yo, k12 (14, 16), ssk, k1, sl m, change to D, k1, k2tog, k8 (10, 12), yo, sl next 2 sts onto cn and hold in front, k2 with D, change to B, k2 from cn, yo, k8 (10, 12), ssk, k1, change to C, k1, k2tog, k22, M1, k2.

Rep Rows 1–8 until piece measures about 15½ (15½, 17½)" (39.5 [39.5, 44.5] cm) from pick-up row, ending with Row 1 or Row 5. Change to A and cont as foll.

ROW 9: (WS) Sl 2 pwise wyf, knit to end.

ROW 10: (RS; Row 2 of patt) Keeping in patt, work 53 (57, 61) sts of left front, sl m, k1, k2tog, k12 (14, 16), yo, k4, yo, k12 (14, 16), ssk, k1, sl m, work 106 (114, 122) sts of back, sl m, k1, k2tog, k12 (14, 16), yo, k4, yo, k12 (14, 16), ssk, k1, sl m, work 53 (57, 61) sts of right front.

Rep Rows 9 and 10 once more. With WS facing, BO all sts kwise—3 garter ridges.

SLEEVES

With A, 16" (40 cm) cir needle, and RS facing, pick up and knit 34 (38, 42) sts along CO row at underarm, place marker (pm), pick up and knit 70 (74, 78) sts evenly spaced around armhole opening—104 (112, 120) sts total. Pm and join for working in rnds.

RND 1: (dec rnd) Knit to 2 sts before m, ssk, sl m, knit to next m, sl m, k2tog—2 sts dec'd.

RND 2: Knit.

Rep Rnds 1 and 2 fifteen (seventeen, nineteen) more times—72 (76, 80) sts rem (2 sts between markers). Pm between these 2 sts to denote beg of rnd; remove other markers. Knit 6 rnds.

DEC RND: K1, k2tog, knit to last 3 sts, ssk, k1—2 sts dec'd.

Dec 1 st each side of marker in this manner every 10th (8th, 8th) rnd 11 (13, 14) more times—48 (48, 50) sts rem. Work even in St st until sleeve measures 17¾" (45 cm) from pick-up rnd, or desired length. Work 7 rnds of garter st (alternate knit 1 rnd, purl 1 rnd), ending with a knit rnd. BO all sts purlwise—4 garter ridges.

FINISHING
Weave in loose ends. Block to measurements.

Neckband
With A, smaller 24" (60 cm) cir needle, and RS facing, pick up and knit 131 sts evenly spaced around neck edge. Knit 1 WS row.

DEC ROW: (RS) K2tog, knit to last 2 sts, ssk—2 sts dec'd.

Rep the last 2 rows once more—127 sts rem. Knit 1 WS row. Cut off A. Join a single strand of D2 and cont as foll.

INC ROW: (RS) Sl 1 pwise wyb, M1, knit to last st, M1, k1—2 sts inc'd.

NEXT ROW: (WS) Sl 1 pwise wyf, purl to end.

Rep the last 2 rows 2 more times—133 sts.

NEXT ROW: (RS) Sl 1 pwise wyb, M1, k6, ssk, k1, join second ball of D2 and BO to last 10 sts, k1, k2tog, k6, M1, k1—10 sts rem each side.

Working each side separately as foll: WS rows: Sl 1 pwise wyf, purl to BO sts; on other side, sl 1 pwise wyf, purl to end. RS rows: Sl 1 pwise wyb, M1, k6, ssk, k1; on other side, sl 1 pwise wyb, k2tog, k6, M1, k1. Rep these 2 rows until piece measures same as center front to lower edge. BO all sts. Lightly steam-press the garment on WS, being careful not to flatten the cables.

With sharp-point sewing needle and thread, sew zipper in place (see Glossary). With yarn threaded on a tapestry needle, sew facings along edges of zipper. Sew neckband facing to WS.

technique: knitting cables

Cables are formed by changing the position of a group of stitches on the needles. Most simple cables involve two, four, six, or eight stitches.

The examples shown here involve a total of four stitches—two groups of two stitches each change position.

Left-Leaning Cable

STEP 1: Knit to the position of the cable, then slip the first two cable stitches onto a cable needle (Figure 1).

STEP 2: Hold the cable needle in front of the work and knit the next two stitches (Figure 2).

STEP 3: Knit the two stitches from the cable needle in the same order that they were slipped (Figure 3).

STEP 4: Knit the remaining stitches (Figure 4).

Right-Leaning Cable

STEP 1: Knit to the position of the cable, then slip the first two cable stitches onto a cable needle and hold the cable needle in back of the work (Figure 1).

STEP 2: Knit the next two stitches (Figure 2).

STEP 3: Knit the two stitches from the cable needle in the same order that they were slipped (Figure 3).

STEP 4: Knit the remaining stitches (Figure 4).

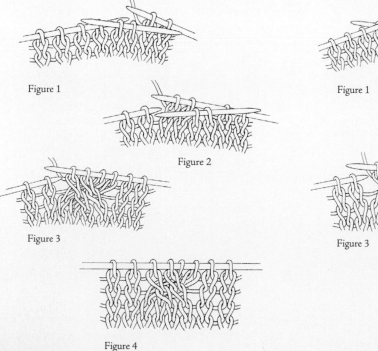

Figure 1

Figure 2

Figure 3

Figure 4

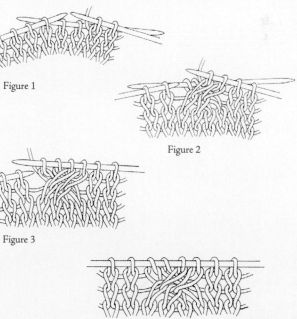

Figure 1

Figure 2

Figure 3

Figure 4

mie's jacket

I designed this jacket and matching cap for my godchild, Mie. The jacket is worked in chevron knitting that begins with a garter-stitch triangle. The zigzag stripes are enhanced by the two stitches that are knitted on right-side rows and slipped on wrong-side rows to give them a bit of surface relief. This is a good project to use up partial balls of yarn leftover from other projects. The more colors, the better.

FINISHED SIZE
Jacket: About 24 (28¾, 33½)" (61 [73, 85] cm) chest circumference. To fit 1 (3, 5) years. Jacket shown measures 28¾" (73 cm). **Cap:** About 15¾ (17)" (40 [43] cm) head circumference. To fit sizes 1–3 (3–5) years. Cap shown measures 17" (43 cm).

YARN
About 150 (200, 250) grams of a main color (MC1) of fingering-weight (#1 Super Fine) yarn, 100 (150, 200) grams of a main color (MC2) of laceweight (#0 Lace) yarn, and a total of about 50 grams of six contrasting colors (A, B, C, D, E, and F) of laceweight yarn.

Shown here: **Alpaca 2** (50% merino, 50% alpaca; 270 yd [247 m]/50 g): #2105 light gray heather (MC1), 3 (4, 5) skeins. **Wool 1** (100% wool; 340 yd [311 m]/50 g): #3s light tan heather (MC2), 2 (3, 4) skeins; #52 plum heather (A), #39s salmon heather (B), #10s light blue heather (C), #16 steel blue (D), #28s coral heather (E), and #40 chartreuse (F), less than 1 skein each (worked with two strands held tog).

NEEDLES
Size U.S. 2 (3 mm): straight, 16" (40 cm) and 24" (60 cm) circular (cir), and set of 4 or 5 double-pointed (dpn). Adjust needle size if necessary to obtain the correct gauge.

NOTIONS
Stitch holders; removable markers; tapestry needle; 14 (16, 18)" (35.5 [40.5, 45.5] cm) separating zipper; sharp-point sewing needle; contrasting sewing thread for basting zipper; matching sewing thread for sewing zipper.

GAUGE
30 stitches and 36 rows = 4" (10 cm) in pattern stitch.

GAUGE SWATCH

Wind two yarn butterflies; one with two strands of A, one with two strands of B held tog.

With one strand each of MC1 and MC2 held tog, CO 4 sts.

ROW 1: (RS) K1, yo, k2, yo, k1—6 sts.
ROW 2: K1, k1 through back loop (tbl; worked into the yo of previous row), sl 2 (see Notes), k1tbl, k1.
ROW 3: [K1, yo] 2 times, k2, [yo, k1] 2 times—10 sts.
ROW 4: [K1, k1tbl] 2 times, sl 2, [k1tbl, k1] 2 times.
ROW 5: K1, yo, k3, yo, k2, yo, k3, yo, k1—14 sts.
ROW 6: K1, k1tbl, k3, k1tbl, sl 2, k1tbl, k3, k1tbl, k1.
ROW 7: K1, yo, k5, yo, k2, yo, k5, yo, k1—18 sts.
ROW 8: K1, k1tbl, k5, k1tbl, sl 2, k1tbl, k5, k1tbl, k1.
ROW 9: K1, yo, k7, yo, k2, yo, k7, yo, k1—22 sts.
ROW 10: K1, k1tbl, k7, k1tbl, sl 2, k1tbl, k7, k1tbl, k1.

Cont in this manner, inc 4 sts every RS row and working the yarnovers as k1tbl on WS rows, until there are 30 sts, ending with a WS row.

NEXT ROW: (RS) K1, k2tog, k11, yo, k2, yo, k11, ssk, k1.
NEXT ROW: (WS) K13, k1tbl, sl 2, k1tbl, k13.

Rep the last 2 rows 3 more times. Work contrast colors, twisting yarn around each other at color changes (see Notes) as foll: **RS rows:** With A, k1, k2tog, k11, M1 (see Glossary), k1, change to B, k1, M1, k11, ssk, k1. **WS rows:** With B, k1, p14, change to A, p14, k1. Rep the last 2 rows 2 more times—6 rows of contrast color. Change to MC1 and MC2 held tog and work as foll: **RS rows:** K1, k2tog, k11, yo, k2, yo, k11, ssk, k1. **WS rows:** K13, k1tbl, sl 2 pwise wyf, k1tbl, k13. Rep the last 2 rows 5 more times, then work 1 more RS row—13 rows total. BO all sts.

Block as described on page 33.

NOTES

+ Work with one strand each of MC1 and MC2 held together; work with two strands of each contrast color held together.

+ The jacket is worked from the top down, beginning at the center back neck.

+ Slip stitches purlwise with yarn in front on wrong-side rows.

+ Use the intarsia method (see page 49) to twist the yarns around each other on the wrong side at color changes to prevent holes.

+ The placement of contrast colors in the sweater worn by the model on pages 114 and 122 and in the gauge swatch opposite is different from the placement in the sample sweater shown photographed flat. The instructions match this sample garment.

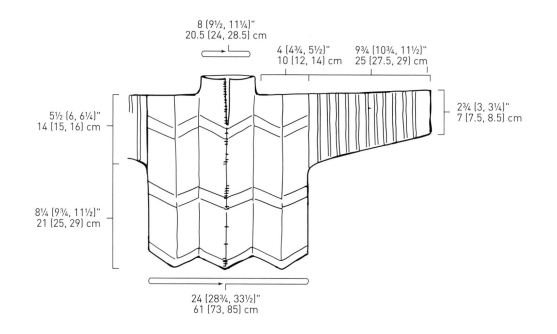

8 (9½, 11¼)"
20.5 (24, 28.5) cm

4 (4¾, 5½)"
10 (12, 14) cm

9¾ (10¾, 11½)"
25 (27.5, 29) cm

5½ (6, 6¼)"
14 (15, 16) cm

2¾ (3, 3¼)"
7 (7.5, 8.5) cm

8¼ (9¾, 11½)"
21 (25, 29) cm

24 (28¾, 33½)"
61 (73, 85) cm

COLLAR

With one strand of each MC1 and MC2 held tog and straight needles, CO 4 sts. Work in chevron patt as for gauge swatch until there are 30 (34, 42) sts for back collar, ending after a WS row. Place sts on holder.

Make a triangle for each front collar as foll: With MC, CO 3 sts.

ROW 1: K1, yo, k1, yo, k1—5 sts.
ROW 2: K1, k1tbl, k1, k1tbl, k1.
ROW 3: K1, yo, k3, yo, k1—7 sts.
ROW 4: K1, k1tbl, k3, k1tbl, k1.
ROW 5: K1, yo, k5, yo, k1—9 sts.
ROW 6: K1, k1tbl, k5, k1tbl, k1.

Cont in this manner, inc 1 st each end of needle every RS row until there are 15 (19, 21) sts, ending with a WS row. Slip sts to holder. Make another triangle to match. Arrange sts on cir needle with RS facing as foll: 15 (19, 21) sts of one triangle, 30 (34, 42) back collar sts, 15 (19, 21) sts of the other triangle—60 (72, 84) sts total. Work in garter st as foll.

ROW 1: (RS) K1, yo, k11 (14, 17), ssk, k2, k2tog, k11 (14, 17), yo, k2, yo, k11 (14, 17), ssk, k2, k2tog, k11 (14, 17), yo, k1.
ROW 2: (WS) K1, k1tbl, k12 (15, 18), sl 2 (see Notes), k12 (15, 18), k1tbl, sl 2, k12 (15, 18), k1tbl, sl 2, k12 (15, 18), k1tbl, k1.

Rep the last 2 rows 6 more times—14 rows total. Place the outermost 15 (18, 21) sts at each side on a holder to work later for front—30 (36, 42) sts rem for back. Place sts on holder.

SHOULDERS (MAKE 4)

With one strand each of MC1 and MC2 held tog and straight needles, CO 4 sts. Work in chevron patt as for gauge swatch until there are 30 (34, 42) sts, ending with a WS row.

Size 28¾" Only

(RS) K16, yo, k2, yo, k16—36 sts. (WS) K16, k1tbl, sl 2 pwise wyf, k1tbl, k16.

All Sizes

Place sts on holder.

BACK

With RS facing, place sts on longer cir needle as foll: 30 (36, 42) shoulder sts, 30 (36, 42) back collar sts, 30 (36, 42) sts from a second shoulder—90 (108, 126) sts total. Work back and forth in garter st as foll.

ROW 1: (RS) K1, k2tog, k11 (14, 17), yo, k2, yo, k11 (14, 17), ssk, *k2, k2tog, k11 (14, 17), yo, k2, yo, k11 (14, 17), ssk; rep from * once, k1.

ROW 2: (WS) K13 (16, 19), k1tbl, sl 2, k1tbl, k12 (15, 18), *sl 2, k12 (15, 18), k1tbl, sl 2, k1tbl, k12 (15, 18); rep from * once, k1.

Rep the last 2 rows until piece measures 2½" (6.5 cm) from joining row, ending with a WS row.

Wind 6 yarn butterflies, each with two strands of a contrast color. Work contrast colors in intarsia, twisting yarn around each other at color changes as foll:

ROW 1: (RS) *With butterfly, k1, k2tog, k11 (14, 17), M1, k1, change to next butterfly, k1, M1, k11 (14, 17), ssk, k1; rep from * 2 times for rem butterflies.

ROW 2: (WS) *With butterfly, k1, p14 (17, 20), change to next butterfly, p14 (17, 20), k1; rep from * 2 times for rem butterflies.

Rep the last 2 rows 2 more times—6 rows of contrast color.

Change to garter st as before and work in patt until piece measures 5½ (6, 6¼)" (14 [15, 16] cm) from joining row, or desired length to underarm. Place all sts on holder.

FRONTS

With RS facing, place 30 (36, 42) sts from one shoulder on longer cir needle, followed by 15 (18, 21) sts of the right front collar, join new yarn, 15 (18, 21) sts of the left front collar, and 30 (36, 42) sts from another shoulder—90 (108, 126) sts total; 45 (54, 63) sts for each front. Join one strand each of MC1 and MC2 and work each front separately back and forth in garter st as foll.

ROW 1: (RS) On right front, k1, k2tog, k11 (14, 17), yo, k2, yo, k11 (14, 17), ssk, k2, k2tog, k11 (14, 17), yo, k1; on left front, k1, yo, k11 (14, 17), ssk, k2, k2tog, k11 (14, 17), yo, k2, yo, k11 (14, 17), ssk, k1.

ROW 2: (WS) On left front, k13 (16, 19), k1tbl, sl 2, k1tbl, k12 (15, 18), sl 2, k12 (15, 18), k1tbl, k1; on right front, k1, k1tbl, k12 (15, 18), sl 2, k12 (15, 18), k1tbl, sl 2, k1tbl, k13 (16, 19).

Rep the last 2 rows until piece measures 2½" (6.5 cm) from joining row, ending with a WS row.

Wind 6 yarn butterflies, each with two strands of a contrast color. Work contrast colors randomly in intarsia, twisting yarn around each other at color changes as foll.

ROW 1: (RS) On right front, with first butterfly, k1, k2tog, k11 (14, 17), M1, k1, change to next butterfly, k1, M1, k11 (14, 17), ssk, k1, change to next butterfly, k1, k2tog, k11 (14, 17), M1, k1; on left front, with next butterfly, k1, M1, k11 (14, 17), ssk, k1, change to next butterfly, k1, k2tog, k11 (14, 17), M1, k1, change to next butterfly, k1, M1, k11 (14, 17), ssk, k1.

ROW 2: (WS) On left front, with last butterfly, k1, p14 (17, 20), change to next butterfly, p15 (18, 21), change to next butterfly, p14 (17, 20), k1; on right front, k1, p14 (17, 20), change to next butterfly, p15 (18, 21), change to next butterfly, p14 (17, 20), k1.

Rep the last 2 rows 2 more times—6 rows of contrast color.

Change to garter st as before and work even in patt until piece measures 5½ (6, 6¼)" (14 [15, 16] cm) from joining row, or desired length to underarm. Place all sts on holder.

LOWER BODY

With RS facing, arrange sts on longer cir needle as foll: 45 (54, 63) left front sts, 90 (108, 126) back sts, 45 (54, 63) right front sts—180 (216, 252) sts total. Work even in patt until piece measures 5½ (6, 6¼)" (14 [15, 16] cm) past the 6 rows of contrast color, ending with a WS row. Wind 12 yarn butterflies in various contrast colors as before. Work contrast colors randomly in intarsia, twisting yarn around each other at color changes as foll:

ROW 1: (RS) With first butterfly, k1, M1, k11 (14, 17), ssk, k1, change to next butterfly, k1, k2tog, k11 (14, 17), M1, k1, *change to next butterfly, k1, M1, k11 (14, 17), ssk, k1, change to next butterfly, k1, k2tog, k11 (14, 17), M1, k1; rep from * 4 more times.

ROW 2: (WS) With last butterfly, k1, p14 (17, 20), *change to next butterfly, p15 (18, 21), change to next butterfly; rep from * 6 more times, change to next butterfly, p14 (17, 20), k1.

Rep the last 2 rows 2 more times—6 rows of contrast color.

Change to garter st as before and work in patt until piece measures 13¾ (15¾, 17¾)" (35 [40, 45] cm) from center back collar or desired total length (keep in mind that length must be ¼" [6 mm] shorter than zipper length). BO all sts.

JOIN FRONTS TO BACK AT SHOULDERS

With MC, dpn, and RS facing, pick up and knit 22 (26, 30) sts along right front shoulder. With another dpn, pick up and knit the same number of sts along right back shoulder. Holding pieces with WS facing tog, use the three-needle method (see Glossary) to BO the sts tog to make a decorative ridge on the RS.

SLEEVES

With MC, shorter cir needle, and RS facing, pick up and knit 64 (70, 76) sts evenly spaced around armhole. Working back and forth, knit 5 rows (3 garter ridges), ending with a WS row. With CC of your choice, work 2 rows in St st. Rep the last 8 rows, working garter st for 6 rows and changing contrast color for 2 rows of St st and *at the same time* beg with the first row of St st, dec 1 st each end of needle as foll: (RS) K1, k2tog, knit to last 3 sts, k2tog, k1—2 sts dec'd. Work 7 rows even. Rep the last 8 rows 10 (11, 12) more times—42 (46, 50) sts rem. Cont in patt until sleeve measures about 9¾ (10¾, 11½)" (25 [27.5, 29] cm) from pick-up row or desired total length, ending with a WS row after working 6 rows of garter st. With RS facing, BO all sts knitwise.

FINISHING

Weave in loose ends. Block to measurements. With MC threaded on a tapestry needle, use the mattress st (see Glossary) to sew sleeve seams.

Neck and Front Facing

With 2 strands of your choice of CC held tog, shorter cir needle, and RS facing, pick up and knit 44 (52, 60) sts evenly spaced around neck opening. Knitting the first and last st of every row, work center 42 (50, 58) sts in St st for 1½" (3.8 cm), ending with a WS row.

NEXT ROW: (RS) Sl 1 pwise with yarn in back (wyb), k10 (12, 14), join 2 more strands of yarn, BO 22 (26, 30) sts, work to end—11 (12, 14) sts rem each side.

Working each side separately, (WS) work 1 row even.

DEC ROW: (RS) Work to 3 sts before BO sts, k2tog, k1; on other side of BO sts, k1, ssk, work to end—1 st dec'd each side.

Work 3 rows even. Rep the last 4 rows 2 (3, 5) more times—8 sts rem each side. Work even for facing until piece is same length as zipper. BO all sts.

Zipper

With sharp-point sewing needle and thread, sew zipper in place (see Glossary). With yarn threaded on a tapestry needle, sew facing to WS of sweater, securely behind zipper and back neck.

Steam-press all seams, including armhole, neck and fronts.

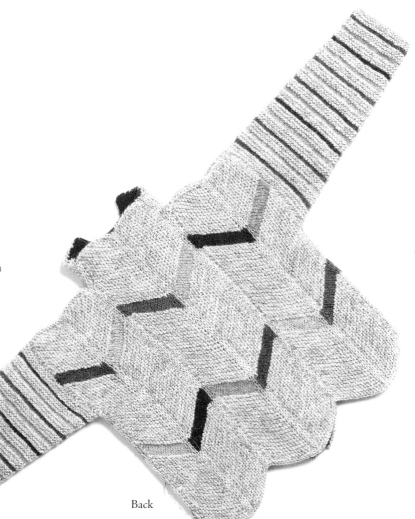

Back

CAP

Make 2 triangles as for gauge swatch until there are a total of 30 sts in each triangle, ending with a WS row.

Size 17" Only

NEXT ROW: (RS) K14, yo, k2, yo, k14—32 sts.

NEXT ROW: (WS) K14, k1tbl, sl 2, k1tbl, k14.

Both sizes:

Place sts on holder.

Join Triangles

With MC1 and MC2 held tog and shorter cir needle, CO 13 (14) sts, work 30 (32) sts of one triangle, use the backward-loop method (see Glossary) to CO 34 (36) sts, work 30 (32) sts of other triangle, CO 13 (14) sts—120 (128) sts total. Work back and forth in garter st as foll.

ROW 1: (RS) K1, yo, k9 (10), ssk, k2, k2tog, k11 (12), yo, k2, yo, k11 (12), ssk, k2, k2tog, k13 (14), yo, k2, yo, k13 (14), ssk, k2, k2tog, k11 (12), yo, k2, yo, k11 (12), ssk, k2, k2tog, k9 (10), yo, k1.

ROW 2: (WS) K1, k1tbl, k10 (11), sl 2 (see Notes), k12

(13), k1tbl, sl 2, k1tbl, k12 (13), sl 2, k14 (15), k1tbl, sl 2, k1tbl, k14 (15), sl 2, k12 (13), k1tbl, sl 2, k1tbl, k12 (13), sl 2, k10 (11), k1tbl, k1.

Rep the last 2 rows 4 more times—3 garter ridges.

Wind 8 yarn butterflies in various colors, each with two strands of your choice of CC. Work contrast colors in intarsia, twisting yarn around each other at color changes as foll.

ROW 1: (RS) With butterfly, k1, M1, k9 (10), ssk, k1, change to next butterfly, k1, k2tog, k11 (12), M1, k1, change to next butterfly, k1, M1, k11 (12), ssk, k1, change to next butterfly, k1, k2tog, k13 (14), M1, k1, change to next butterfly, k1, M1, k13 (14), ssk, k1, change to next butterfly, k1, k2tog, k11 (12), M1, k1, change to next butterfly, k1, M1, k11 (12), ssk, k1, change to next butterfly, k1, k2tog, k9 (10), M1, k1.

ROW 2: (WS) With butterfly, k11 (12), ssk, k1, change to next butterfly, k1, k2tog, k13 (14), change to next butterfly, k13 (14), ssk, k1, change to next butterfly, k1, k2tog, k15 (16), change to next butterfly, k15 (16), ssk, k1, change to next butterfly, k1, k2tog, k13 (14), change to next butterfly, k13 (14), ssk, k1, change to next butterfly, k1, k2tog, k11 (12).

Rep the last 2 rows 2 more times—6 rows of contrast color. With MC, work 6 rows in garter st as previously established, ending with a WS row.

DEC ROW: (RS) Cont in garter st, but, where you had previously worked k2tog, work k3tog and where you had previously worked ssk, work sssk (see Glossary)—8 sts dec'd.

Dec 8 sts every other row in this manner until just the slipped sts rem. For a longer, pointed top, work a few more rows over rem sts. Cut yarn, leaving an 8" (20.5 cm) tail, thread tail through rem sts, pull tight to gather sts, and secure on WS.

FINISHING

With MC threaded on a tapestry needle, use the mattress st (see Glossary) to sew the seam.

Earflaps

With CC of your choice, straight needles, and begin at the point before the seam, pick up and knit 7 (8) sts to the seam, then 7 (8) sts to the other point—14 (16) sts total. Mark the 2 center sts with a removable marker. Working back and forth in garter st, dec 1 st (k2tog) each side of marked sts every RS row until 4 sts rem. Remove markers and work 1 WS row even. On the next row (RS), [k2tog] 2 times—2 sts rem. BO rem sts.

Make the other earflap the same way but with a different contrast color and on the opposite side of the hat. Weave in loose ends.

Edging

With a third CC, shorter cir needle, and RS facing, pick up and knit 31 (33) sts along each earflap, and 28 (30) sts along each flat edge—118 (122) sts total. Knit 1 (WS) row. With RS facing, BO all sts knitwise.

Weave in loose ends. Make a pom-pom (see Glossary) and sew top of hat.

waves

FINISHED SIZE
About 38½ (44½)" (98 [113] cm)
bust circumference. Sweater shown
measures 38½" (98 cm).

YARN
About 100 (150) grams of a main color
(A) of fingering-weight (#1 Super Fine)
yarn and about 100 (150) grams of a
main color (B) of a different fingering-
weight yarn.

Shown here: **Bomuld** (100% cotton;
228 yd [208 m]/50 g): #10 light blue
(A), 2 (3) skeins. **Bomulin** (75% cotton,
25% linen; 228 yd [208 m]/50 g): #1000
natural (B), 2 (3) skeins.

NEEDLES
Size U.S. 2 (3 mm): straight. Adjust
needle size if necessary to obtain the
correct gauge.

NOTIONS
Tapestry needle.

GAUGE
24 stitches and 52 rows = 4" (10 cm) in
pattern stitch.

This little summer top is called Waves because it is worked in a honeycomb technique. As for many knitting motifs, this one is derived from a weaving technique. The design is made simply by letting some stitches "rest" before knitting them a few rows later. This pulls in those stitches in relation to the others. The top is knitted with a combination of linen and cotton yarns. After knitting the gauge swatch, I decided that I preferred the look of "wrong" and used it as the "right" side of the garment. If you seam the top carefully, either side can face outward. The back and front are identical. The neck and shoulders are shaped with short-rows.

NOTES

+ For the top shown here, I designated what would normally be considered the wrong side of the pattern as the right side. Choose whichever side you prefer as the "right" side. The gauge swatch is shown (and written for) what would normally be considered the right side; the sweater pattern is written for the right side to be what would normally be the considered the wrong side.

+ The front and back are identical and each are worked sideways and seamed at the sides.

+ Instead of binding off and sewing the pieces together, you can use the three-needle method (see Glossary) to bind-off the last row of stitches together with stitches picked up along the cast-on edge of the opposite piece.

GAUGE SWATCH

With one strand each of A and B held tog, CO 35 sts. Knit 3 rows—2 garter ridges. Work short-rows as foll.

ROW 1: (RS) K1 with A and B held tog, drop A and with B, k12, turn work.

ROW 2: With B, yo, p10, k3 (edge sts; knit every row).

ROW 3: K1 with A and B held tog, drop A and with B, k12, k2tog (yo and next st), k1, *sl 2 pwise with yarn in back (wyb), k6; rep from * to last 4 sts, sl 2 pwise wyb, k2.

ROWS 4, 6, AND 8: With B, k1, p1, *sl 2 pwise with yarn in front (wyf), p6; rep from * to last 17 sts, sl 2 pwise wyf, p12, k3.

ROWS 5 AND 7: K1 with A and B held tog, drop A and with B, k15, *sl 2 pwise wyb, k6; repeat from * to last 4 sts, sl 2 pwise wyb, k2.

ROWS 9–12: With A and B held tog, knit 4 rows—2 garter ridges.

ROW 13: Rep Row 1.

ROW 14: Rep Row 2.

ROW 15: K1 with A and B held tog, drop A and with B, k12, k2tog, k5, *sl 2 pwise wyb; rep from * to end.

ROWS 16, 18, AND 20: With B, k1, p5, *sl 2 pwise wyf, p6; rep from * to last 13 sts, p10, k3.

ROWS 17 AND 19: K1 with A and B held tog, drop A and with B, k18, *sl 2 pwise wyb, k6; rep from * to end.

ROWS 21–24: With A and B held tog, knit 4 rows—2 garter ridges.

Rep Rows 1–24 once more.

Block swatch as described on page 33.

FRONT

Wind a small butterfly (see page 49) of A so that both A and B can be worked tog at the selvedge. With A and B held tog, CO 68 (76) sts. Knit 3 rows—2 garter ridges.

ROW 1: (WS) With A and B held tog, k3, drop A and with B, *k6, sl 2 pwise wyb; rep from *6 (7) more times, k6, then k3 with A and B held tog.

ROW 2: K3 with A and B, drop A and with B, *p6, sl 2 pwise wyf; rep from * 6 (7) more times, p6, then k3 with A and B held tog.

ROWS 3 AND 5: Rep Row 1.

ROWS 4 AND 6: Rep Row 2.

ROW 7: (WS) With A and B held tog, knit 1 row, then use the backward-loop method (see Glossary) to CO 45 (52) more sts—113 (128) sts total.

Knit 3 rows—2 garter ridges.

Shape Left Armhole

Cont working short-rows as foll.

SHORT-ROW 1: (WS) K3 with A and B held tog, drop A and with B, k2, *sl 2 pwise wyb, k6; rep from * 7 (8) more times, k1, turn work—70 (78) sts worked.

SHORT-ROWS 2, 4, AND 6: Yo, purl to first set of slipped sts, *sl 2 pwise wyf, p6; rep from * to last set of slipped sts, sl 2 pwise wyf, purl to last 3 sts, k3 with A and B held tog.

SHORT-ROWS 3 AND 5: Work as for Short-row 1 to yo, k2tog (yo plus next st), k1, turn—2 more sts worked; 74 (82) sts worked after Short-row 5.

SHORT-ROWS 7 AND 9: With A and B held tog, knit to yo, k2tog, k1, turn—2 sts more sts worked; 78 (86) sts worked after Short-row 9.

ROWS 8 AND 10: With A and B held tog, yo, knit to end.

ROWS 11, 13, AND 15: With A and B held tog, k3, drop A and with B, *k6, sl 2 pwise wyb; rep from * 8 (9) more times, knit to yo, k2tog, k1, turn—2 more sts worked; 84 (92) sts worked after Row 15.

ROWS 12, 14, AND 16: Rep Short-row 2.

ROWS 17 AND 19: Rep Short-row 7—88 (96) sts worked after Short-row 19.

ROWS 18 AND 20: Rep Short-row 8.

Size 38½" (98 cm)

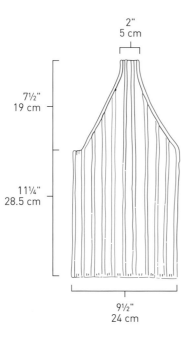

2"
5 cm

7½"
19 cm

11¼"
28.5 cm

9½"
24 cm

Size 44½" (113 cm)

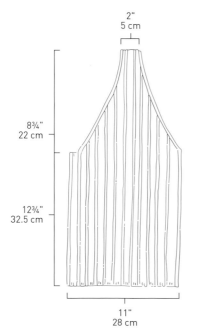

2"
5 cm

8¾"
22 cm

12¾"
32.5 cm

11"
28 cm

ROW 21: With A and B held tog, k3, drop A and with B, k2, *sl 2 pwise wyb, k6; rep from * 9 (10) more times, knit to yo, k2tog, k1, turn—2 more sts worked; 90 (98) sts worked after Row 21.

Rep Short-rows 2–21 once more and *at the same time* on Short-rows 11, 13, and 15, work patt rep a total of 11 (12) times, and on Short-row 21, work patt rep a total of 13 (14) times, before ending with yo, k2tog, k1, turn—110 (118) sts worked after second rep of Short-row 21.

Size 44½" Only
Rep Short-rows 2–11 once more—128 sts worked.

Shape Left Strap
ROW 1: (RS) With B, purl to first set of slipped sts, *sl 2 pwise wyf, p6; rep from * to last set of slipped sts, sl 2 pwise wyf, purl to last 3 sts, k3 with A and B held tog.
ROW 2: With A and B held tog, k3, drop A and with B, k2 (6), sl 2 pwise wyb, *k6, sl 2 pwise wyb; rep from * 11 (13) more times, k7 (5).

Rep Rows 1 and 2 once more, then rep Row 1 once more. With A and B held tog, knit 4 rows.

NEXT ROW: (WS) With A and B held tog, k3, drop A and with B, k6 (2), sl 2 pwise wyb, *k6, sl 2 pwise wyb; rep from * 11 (14) more times, k3 (1).
NEXT ROW: Rep Row 1.

Rep the last 2 rows 2 more times. With A and B held tog, knit 4 rows. Rep Row 2, then rep Rows 1 and 2 two times, then rep Row 1 once more.

Shape Left Neck

Cont working short-rows as foll.

SHORT-ROW 1: (WS) With A and B held tog, knit to last 4 (1) st(s), turn work—109 (127) sts worked.

SHORT-ROW 2: With A and B held tog, yo, knit to end.

SHORT-ROW 3: With A and B held tog, knit to 2 sts before yo, turn—107 (125) sts worked.

SHORT-ROW 4: Rep Short-row 2.

Cont for your size as foll.

Size 38½" Only

SHORT-ROW 5: (WS) With A and B held tog, k3, drop A and with B, *k6, sl 2 pwise wyb; rep from * 11 times, knit to 2 sts before yo, turn work—105 sts worked.

SHORT-ROW 6: With B, yo, purl to first set of slipped sts, *sl 2 pwise wyf, p6; rep from * to last set of slipped sts, sl 2 pwise wyf, purl to last 3 sts, k3 with A and B held tog.

SHORT-ROWS 7 AND 9: Rep Short-row 5—101 sts worked after Short-row 9.

SHORT-ROWS 8 AND 10: Rep Short-row 6.

SHORT-ROWS 11 AND 13: Rep Short-row 3—97 sts worked after Short-row 13.

SHORT-ROWS 12 AND 14: Rep Short-row 4.

SHORT-ROW 15: (WS) With A and B held tog, k3, drop A and with B, k2, sl 2 pwise wyb, *k6, sl 2 pwise wyb; rep from * 9 more times, knit to 2 sts before yo, turn—95 sts worked.

SHORT-ROW 16: With B, yo, purl to first set of slipped sts, *sl 2 pwise wyf, p6; rep from * to last set of slipped sts, sl 2 pwise wyf, purl to last 3 sts, k3 with A and B held tog.

SHORT-ROWS 17 AND 19: Rep Short-row 15—91 sts worked after Short-row 19.

SHORT-ROWS 18 AND 20: Rep Short-row 16.

SHORT-ROWS 21 AND 23: Rep Short-row 3—87 sts worked after Short-row 23.

SHORT-ROWS 22 AND 24: Rep Short-row 2.

SHORT-ROWS 25, 27, AND 29: With A and B held tog, k3, drop A and with B, *k6, sl 2 pwise wyb; rep from * 8 (12) times, knit to 2 sts before yo, turn—81 sts worked after Short-row 29.

SHORT-ROW 26, 28, AND 30: With B, yo, purl to first set of slipped sts, *sl 2 pwise wyf, p6; rep from * to last set of slipped sts, sl 2 pwise wyf, purl to last 3 sts, k3 with A and B held tog.

SHORT-ROWS 31 AND 33: Rep Short-row 3—77 sts worked after Short-row 33.

SHORT-ROWS 32 AND 34: Rep Short-row 2.

Size 44½" Only

SHORT-ROW 5: (WS) K3 with A and B held tog, drop A and with B alone, k2, sl 2 pwise wyb, *k6, sl 2 pwise wyb; rep from * 12 more times, knit to 2 sts before yo, turn—123 sts worked.

SHORT-ROW 6: With B, yo, purl to first set of slipped sts, *sl 2 pwise wyf, p6; rep from * to last set of slipped sts, sl 2 pwise wyf, purl to last 3 sts, k3 with A and B held tog.

SHORT-ROWS 7 AND 9: Rep Short-row 5—119 sts worked after Short-row 9.

SHORT-ROWS 8 AND 10: Rep Short-row 6.

SHORT-ROWS 11 AND 13: Rep Short-row 3—115 sts worked after Short-row 13.

SHORT-ROWS 12 AND 14: Rep Short-row 2.

SHORT-ROWS 15, 17, AND 19: With A and B held tog, k3, drop A and with B, *k6, sl 2 pwise wyb; rep from * 12 times, knit to 2 sts before yo, turn—109 sts worked after Short-row 19.

SHORT-ROWS 16, 18, AND 20: With B, yo, purl to first set of slipped sts, *sl 2 pwise wyf, p6; rep from * to last set of slipped sts, sl 2 pwise wyf, purl to last 3 sts, k3 with A and B held tog.

SHORT-ROWS 21 AND 23: Rep Short-row 3—105 sts worked after Short-row 23.

SHORT-ROWS 22 AND 24: Rep Short-row 2.

Rep Short-rows 5–24 once more—85 sts worked after second rep of Row 24.

Both Sizes

SHORT-ROW 1: (WS) With A and B held tog, k3, drop A and with B, k2, sl 2 pwise wyb, *k6, sl 2 pwise wyb; rep from * 6 (9) more times, knit to 2 sts before yo, turn—75 (83) sts worked.

SHORT-ROW 2: With, yo, purl to first set of slipped sts, *sl 2 pwise wyf, p6; rep from * to last set of slipped sts, sl 2 pwise wyf, purl to last 3 sts, k3 with A and B held tog.

SHORT-ROWS 3 AND 5: Rep Short-row 1—71 (79) sts worked after Short-row 5.

SHORT-ROWS 4 AND 6: Rep Short-row 2.

ROW 7: With A and B held tog, knit to yo, *k2tog (yo and next st), k1; rep from * to end—113 (128) sts.

ROWS 8 AND 9: With A and B held tog, knit.

ROW 10: (RS) BO 45 (52) sts knitwise, knit to end—68 (76) sts rem.

ROW 11: With A and B held tog, k3, drop A and with B, *k6, sl 2 pwise wyb; rep from * 6 (7) more times, k6, then k3 with A and B held tog.

ROW 12: With A and B held tog, k3, drop A and with B, *p6, sl 2 pwise wyf; rep from * 6 (7) more times, p6, k3 with A and B held tog.

ROW 13: With A and B held tog, knit 1 row, then use the backward-loop method to CO 45 (52) more sts—113 (128) sts total.

Knit 3 rows—2 garter ridges.

Shape Right Neck

Cont working short-rows as foll to shape right neck.

SHORT-ROW 1: (WS) K3 with A and B held tog, drop A and with B, k2, *sl 2 pwise wyb, k6; rep from * 7 (8) more times, k1, turn work—70 (78) sts worked.

SHORT-ROWS 2, 4, AND 6: Yo, purl to first set of slipped sts, *sl 2 pwise wyf, p6; rep from * to last set of slipped sts, sl 2 pwise wyf, purl to last 3 sts, k3 with A and B held tog.

SHORT-ROWS 3 AND 5: Work as for Short-row 1 to yo, k2tog (yo plus next st), k1, turn—2 more sts worked; 74 (82) sts worked after Short-row 5.

SHORT-ROWS 7 AND 9: With A and B held tog, knit to yo, k2tog, k1, turn—2 sts more sts worked; 78 (86) sts worked after Short-row 9.

ROWS 8 AND 10: With A and B held tog, yo, knit to end.

ROWS 11, 13, AND 15: With A and B held tog, k3, drop A and with B, *k6, sl 2 pwise wyb; rep from * 8 (9) more times, knit to yo, k2tog, k1, turn—2 more sts worked; 84 (92) sts worked after Row 15.

ROWS 12, 14, AND 16: Rep Short-row 2.

ROWS 17 AND 19: Rep Short-row 7—88 (96) sts worked after Short-row 19.

ROWS 18 AND 20: Rep Short-row 8.

ROW 21: With A and B held tog, k3, drop A and with B, k2, *sl 2 pwise wyb, k6; rep from * 9 (10) more times, knit to yo, k2tog, k1, turn—2 more sts worked; 90 (98) sts worked after Row 21.

Rep Short-rows 2–21 once more and *at the same time* on Short-rows 11, 13, and 15, work patt rep a total of 11 (12) times, and on Short-row 21, work patt rep a total of 13 (14) times, before ending with yo, k2tog, k1, turn—110 (118) sts worked after second rep of Short-row 21.

Size 44½" Only

Rep Short-rows 2–11 once more—128 sts worked.

Shape Right Strap

ROW 1: (RS) With B, purl to first set of slipped sts, *sl 2 pwise wyf, p6; rep from * to last set of slipped sts, sl 2 pwise wyf, purl to last 3 sts, k3 with A and B held tog.

ROW 2: With A and B held tog, k3, drop A and with B, k2 (6), sl 2 pwise wyb, *k6, sl 2 pwise wyb; rep from * 11 (13) more times, k7 (5).

Rep Rows 1 and 2 once more, then rep Row 1 once more. With A and B held tog, knit 4 rows.

NEXT ROW: With A and B held tog, k3, drop A and with B, k6 (2), sl 2 pwise wyb, *k6, sl 2 pwise wyb; rep from * 11 (14) more times, k3 (1).

NEXT ROW: Rep Row 1.

Rep the last 2 rows 2 more times. With A and B held tog, knit 4 rows. Rep Row 2, then rep Rows 1 and 2 two times, then rep Row 1 once more.

Shape Right Armhole:

Cont working short-rows as foll.

SHORT-ROW 1: (WS) With A and B held tog, knit to last 4 (1) st(s), turn work—109 (127) sts worked.

SHORT-ROW 2: With A and B held tog, yo, knit to end.

SHORT-ROW 3: With A and B held tog, knit to 2 sts before yo, turn—107 (125) sts worked.

SHORT-ROW 4: Rep Short-row 2.

Cont for your size as foll.

Size 38½" Only

SHORT-ROW 5: (WS) With A and B held tog, k3, drop A and with B, *k6, sl 2 pwise wyb; rep from * 11 times, knit to 2 sts before yo, turn work—105 sts worked.

SHORT-ROW 6: With B, yo, purl to first set of slipped sts, *sl 2 pwise wyf, p6; rep from * to last set of slipped sts, sl 2 pwise wyf, purl to last 3 sts, k3 with A and B held tog.

SHORT-ROWS 7 AND 9: Rep Short-row 5—101 sts worked after Short-row 9.

SHORT-ROWS 8 AND 10: Rep Short-row 6.

SHORT-ROWS 11 AND 13: Rep Short-row 3—97 sts worked after Short-row 13.

SHORT-ROWS 12 AND 14: Rep Short-row 4.

SHORT-ROW 15: (WS) With A and B held tog, k3, drop A and with B, k2, sl 2 pwise wyb, *k6, sl 2 pwise wyb; rep from * 9 more times, knit to 2 sts before yo, turn—95 sts worked.

SHORT-ROW 16: With B, yo, purl to first set of slipped sts, *sl 2 pwise wyf, p6; rep from * to last set of slipped sts, sl 2 pwise wyf, purl to last 3 sts, k3 with A and B held tog.

SHORT-ROWS 17 AND 19: Rep Short-row 15—91 sts worked after Short-row 19.

SHORT-ROWS 18 AND 20: Rep Short-row 16.

SHORT-ROWS 21 AND 23: Rep Short-row 3—87 sts worked after Short-row 23.

SHORT-ROWS 22 AND 24: Rep Short-row 2.

SHORT-ROWS 25, 27, AND 29: With A and B held tog, k3, drop A and with B, *k6, sl 2 pwise wyb; rep from * 8 (12) times, knit to 2 sts before yo, turn—81 sts worked after Short-row 29.

SHORT-ROWS 26, 28, AND 30: With B, yo, purl to first set of slipped sts, *sl 2 pwise wyf, p6; rep from * to last set of slipped sts, sl 2 pwise wyf, purl to last 3 sts, k3 with A and B held tog.

SHORT-ROWS 31 AND 33: Rep Short-row 3—77 sts worked after Short-row 33.

SHORT-ROWS 32 AND 34: Rep Short-row 2.

Size 44½" Only

SHORT-ROW 5: (WS) K3 with A and B held tog, drop A and with B alone, k2, sl 2 pwise wyb, *k6, sl 2 pwise wyb; rep from * 12 more times, knit to 2 sts before yo, turn—123 sts worked.

SHORT-ROW 6: With B, yo, purl to first set of slipped sts, *sl 2 pwise wyf, p6; rep from * to last set of slipped sts, sl 2 pwise wyf, purl to last 3 sts, k3 with A and B held tog.

SHORT-ROWS 7 AND 9: Rep Short-row 5—119 sts worked after Short-row 9.

SHORT-ROWS 8 AND 10: Rep Short-row 6.

SHORT-ROWS 11 AND 13: Rep Short-row 3—115 sts worked after Short-row 13.

SHORT-ROWS 12 AND 14: Rep Short-row 2.

SHORT-ROWS 15, 17, AND 19: With A and B held tog, k3, drop A and with B, *k6, sl 2 pwise wyb; rep from * 12 times, knit to 2 sts before yo, turn—109 sts worked after Short-row 19.

SHORT-ROWS 16, 18, AND 20: With B, yo, purl to first set of slipped sts, *sl 2 pwise wyf, p6; rep from * to last set of slipped sts, sl 2 pwise wyf, purl to last 3 sts, k3 with A and B held tog.

SHORT-ROWS 21 AND 23: Rep Short-row 3—105 sts worked after Short-row 23.

SHORT-ROWS 22 AND 24: Rep Short-row 2.

Rep Short-rows 5–24 once more—85 sts worked after second rep of Row 24.

Both Sizes

SHORT-ROW 1: (WS) With A and B held tog, k3, drop A and with B, k2, sl 2 pwise wyb, *k6, sl 2 pwise wyb; rep from * 6 (9) more times, knit to 2 sts before yo, turn—75 (83) sts worked.

SHORT-ROW 2: With, yo, purl to first set of slipped sts, *sl 2 pwise wyf, p6; rep from * to last set of slipped sts, sl 2 pwise wyf, purl to last 3 sts, k3 with A and B held tog.

SHORT-ROWS 3 AND 5: Rep Short-row 1—71 (79) sts worked after Short-row 5.

SHORT-ROWS 4 AND 6: Rep Short-row 2.

ROW 7: With A and B held tog, knit to yo, *k2tog (yo and next st), k1; rep from * to end—113 (128) sts.

ROWS 8 AND 9: With A and B held tog, knit.

ROW 10: (RS) BO 45 (52) sts knitwise, knit to end—68 (76) sts rem.

ROW 11: With A and B held tog, k3, drop A and with B, *k6, sl 2 pwise wyb; rep from * 6 (7) more times, k6, then k3 with A and B held tog.

ROW 12: With A and B held tog, k3, drop A and with B, *p6, sl 2 pwise wyf; rep from * 6 (7) more times, p6, k3 with A and B held tog.

Rep Rows 11 and 12 two more times. With A and B held tog, knit 4 rows—2 garter ridges. BO all sts knitwise.

BACK

Work as front.

FINISHING

Block pieces to measurements. Weave in loose ends. With yarn threaded on a tapestry needle, use the mattress st (see Glossary) to sew front to back at sides. Sew shoulder seams.

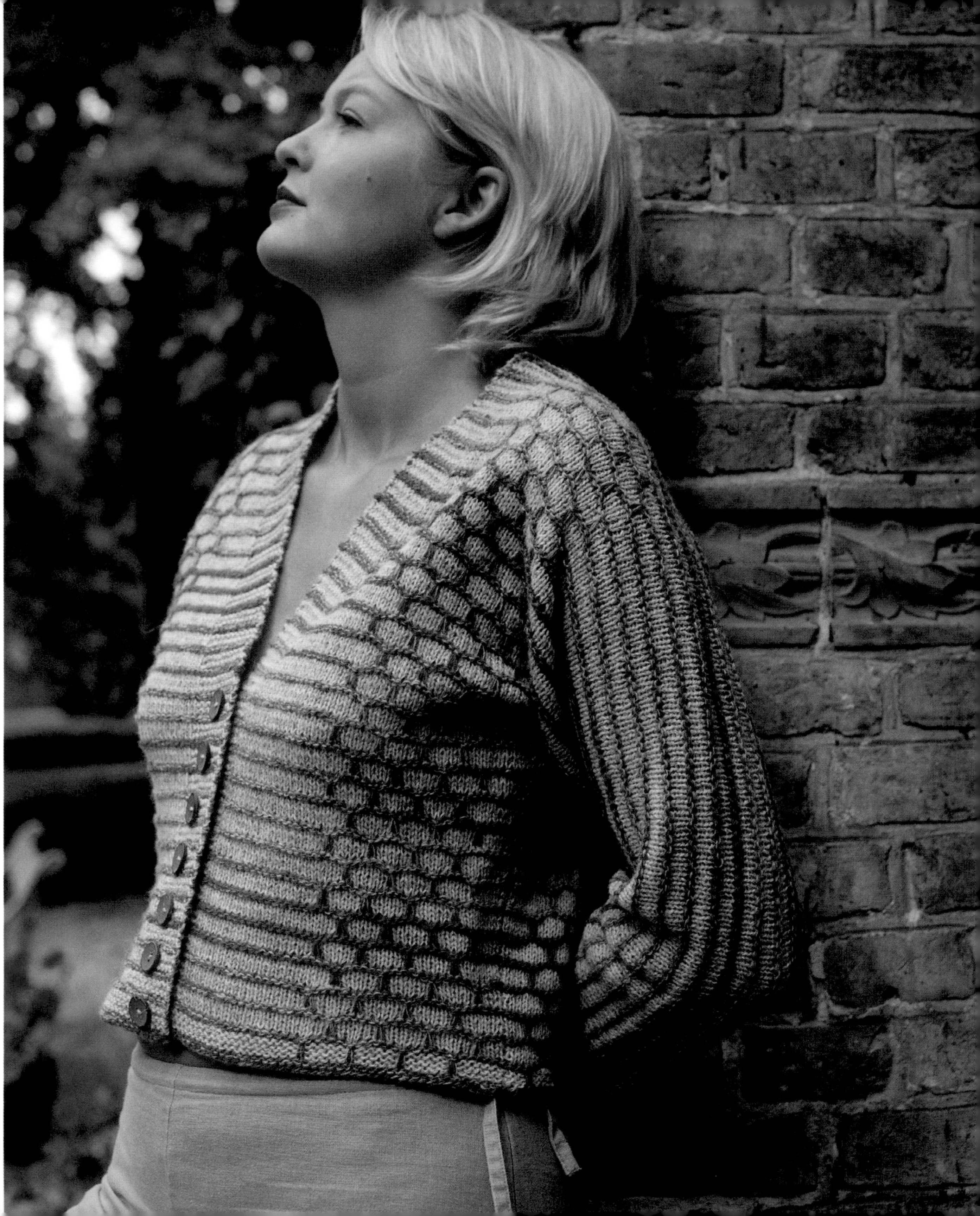

honey

Honey, like the Waves top on page 124, is worked in a honeycomb pattern. However, Waves has four rows in garter stitch and two "resting" stitches, while Honey features two rows in garter stitch and only one "resting" stitch. This version of the pattern makes a six-sided figure like the cells in a honeycomb. I have also combined this design with stripes. All in all, this is an exciting pattern to experiment with. Try using a thinner yarn for the background than for the pattern.

FINISHED SIZE
About 41½ (46)" (106 [117] cm) bust circumference, buttoned. Sweater shown measures 41½" (106 cm).

YARN
About 150 grams of a main color (MC1) of fingering weight (#1 Super Fine), about 150 grams of a main color (MC2) of laceweight (#0 Lace) yarn, and about 200 grams total of seven contrasting colors (CC1, CC2, CC3, CC4, CC5, CC6, and CC7) of laceweight yarn.

Shown here: **Alpaca 2** (50% merino, 50% alpaca; 270 yd [247 m]/50 g): #201 tan heather (MC1), 3 skeins. **Wool 1** (100% wool; 340 yd [311 m]/50 g): #6s tan heather (MC2), 3 skeins; #8s dark brown heather (CC1), #7s medium brown heather (CC2), #16 steel blue (CC3), #23s khaki heather (CC4), #39s salmon heather (CC5), #1s rust heather (CC6), and #52s plum heather (CC7), less than 1 skein each (worked with two strands held tog).

NEEDLES
Size U.S. 4 (3.5 mm). Adjust needle size if necessary to obtain the correct gauge.

NOTIONS
Stitch holders; removable marker; tapestry needle; seven ¾" (2 cm) buttons.

GAUGE
21 stitches and 38 rows = 4" (10 cm) in honeycomb pattern; 19 stitches and 38 rows = 4" (10 cm) in garter-ridge pattern.

GAUGE SWATCH

With 3 random strands of CC held tog (referred to as CC), CO 19 sts. Knit 1 row. Change to 1 strand each of MC1 and MC2 held tog (referred to as MC).

ROW 1: (RS) K3, *sl 1 pwise with yarn in back (wyb), k5; rep from * to last 4 sts, sl 1 pwise wyb, k3.

ROW 2: Work as Row 1, but slip sts pwise with yarn in front (wyf).

ROWS 3–6: Rep Rows 1 and 2 two times.

ROWS 7 AND 8: With CC, knit.

ROW 9: With MC, k1, *k5, sl 1 pwise wyb; rep from * to last 6 sts, k6.

ROW 10: K1, *p5, sl 1 pwise wyf; rep from * to last 6 sts, p5, k1.

ROWS 11 AND 12: Rep Rows 9 and 10 once.

ROWS 13 AND 14: With CC, knit.

ROW 15: With MC, rep Row 1.

ROW 16: K1, p2, *sl 1 pwise wyf, p5; rep from * to last 4 sts, sl 1 pwise wyf, p2, k1.

ROWS 17 AND 18: Rep Rows 15 and 16 once.

ROWS 19 AND 20: With CC, knit.

Rep Rows 9–20 once. BO all sts.

Block as described on page 33.

BACK

With 3 random strands CC held tog (referred to as CC), CO 85 (97) sts. Knit 1 row. Change to 1 strand each of MC1 and MC2 held tog (referred to as MC). Rows 1–8 as for gauge swatch—piece measures about 1" (4 cm).

Increase for Body

INC ROW: (RS; Row 9 of patt) K1 (edge st), M1 (see Glossary), work in patt to last st, M1, k1 (edge st)—2 sts inc'd.

Inc 1 st each end of needle in this manner every 12th (14th) row 7 more times, working new sts in stripe patt (i.e., do not add more "cells")—101 (113) sts. Work even in patt (rep Rows 9–20) until there are a total of 16 (18) cells (98 [110] rows), ending with 2 rows of CC (Row 14 of patt)—piece measures 10¼ (11½)" (26 [29] cm) from CO.

Increase for Sleeves

Use the backward-loop method (see Glossary) to CO 5 sts at the end of every row 30 times (15 times each end)—75 sts inc'd for each sleeve; 251 (263) sts total. Working the first and last 5 sts in garter st (knit every row) and working the first st of every RS row with MC1, MC2, and CC held tog, cont working the cell patt along the center as established and work the sides and sleeves in stripes until 13 (14) cells (78 [84] rows) have been worked from the beg of sleeve incs, ending with 1 (RS) row of CC—piece measures about 8¾ (9¼)" (22 [23.5] cm) from beg of sleeve incs.

Shape Neck and Divide for Fronts

(WS) Mark the center 31 sts. Cont in patt, work to marked center sts, join new yarn, work marked sts, then place these 31 sts on a holder, work to end—110 (116) sts rem each side. Place a removable marker in fabric at each cuff edge to denote center row of sleeve and shoulder line. Working each side separately, cont as foll:

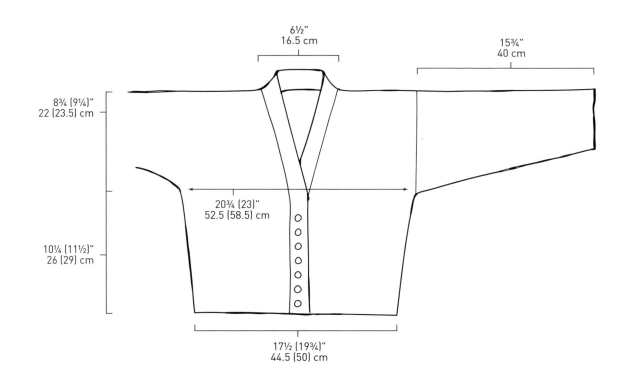

6½"
16.5 cm

15¾"
40 cm

8¾ (9¼)"
22 (23.5) cm

20¾ (23)"
52.5 (58.5) cm

10¼ (11½)"
26 (29) cm

17½ (19¾)"
44.5 (50) cm

RIGHT FRONT

NOTE: The front neck and sleeve are shaped at the same time as buttonholes are introduced; read all the way through the foll section before proceeding. (RS) With MC, cont in patt, and at the neck edge, use the backward-loop method to CO 10 new sts for neck edging—120 (126) sts total. Working the 10 edging sts in garter st, cont in patt for 3 more rows, ending with WS Row 12 (18) of patt.

Shape Neck

INC ROW: (RS) Work in patt to last 10 sts, M1, k10—1 neck st inc'd.

Work 5 rows even in patt. Rep the last 6 rows 14 more times, working new sts in stripes (i.e., do not work cells on new sts). *At the same time* when 8 (9) cells (48 [54] rows) have been worked from cuff marker, ending with a WS row, dec for sleeve and body as foll.

Decrease for Right Sleeve and Body

Keeping in patt, BO 5 sts at cuff edge (beg of RS rows) 15 times to complete sleeve. Cont shaping neck, work 3 (5) more rows, ending with a WS row.

DEC ROW: (RS) K1, ssk, work in patt to end—1 body st dec'd.

Work 11 (13) rows even. Rep the last 12 (14) rows 7 more times. *At the same time* after 15 sts have been inc'd for neck at center front, work 9 rows, ending with WS Row 10 (16) of patt. Make buttonholes next row, then every 12th row 5 times as foll.

BUTTONHOLE ROW: (RS) Work in patt to the last 10 edging sts, k2, BO 2 sts, knit to end.

On the next row, use the backward-loop method to CO 2 sts over the gap made by the BO sts on the previous row. Rep buttonhole row every 12th row 5 more times, then work even in patt until front is the same length as back (16 [18] cells from sleeve), working MC in garter st for the last 6 rows of cells (to match back), and ending with 2 rows of CC—53 (59) sts rem after all shaping is completed.

Neckband

With RS facing, slip 31 held back neck sts on one needle as if to work a RS row. With other needle, RS facing, and 3 random strands of CC held tog, pick up and knit 10 sts from the right front neck edging, slip last st to left needle and knit tog with first st of back neck, turn, k10. Alternating 4 rows of garter st with MC and 2 rows of garter st in CC, cont working over these 10 neckband sts, working every RS row as k1 with both MC and CC, then with working yarn k8, k2tog (last st of neck edging with first st of back neck) until all of the sts from back neck have been joined, ending with 2 rows of CC—10 sts rem. Do not break yarn.

LEFT FRONT

NOTE: For the left front, work the first st of every RS row with MC1, MC2, and CC yarns held tog, then cont across in patt with working yarn. (RS) Cont with MC, k10 edging (neckband) sts, then work across left front in patt—120 (126) sts total. Work 3 more rows, working neck and cuff edging sts in garter st, ending with WS row 12 (18) of pattern stitch.

Shape Neck

INC ROW: (RS) K10, M1, work in patt to end—1 neck st inc'd.

Work 5 rows even. Rep the last 6 rows 15 more times, working new sts in stripes. *At the same time* when 8 (9) cells (47 [53] rows) have been worked from cuff marker, end with a RS row.

Decrease for Left Sleeve and Body

Keeping in patt, BO 5 sts at cuff edge (beg of WS rows) 15 times to complete sleeve. Cont shaping neck, work 4 (6) more rows, ending with a WS row.

DEC ROW: (RS) Work in patt to last 3 sts, k2tog, k1—1 body st dec'd.

Work 11 (13) rows even. Rep the last 12 (14) rows 7 more times—53 (59) sts rem after all shaping has been completed. Work in patt until the front is the same length as back, working the MC in garter st for the last 6 rows of cells, and ending with 2 rows of CC.

FINISHING

Weave in loose ends. Block to measurements. With yarn threaded on a tapestry needle, use the mattress st (see Glossary) to sew sleeve and side seams. Sew buttons to left front, opposite buttonholes.

dashes

||||||||||||||||||||||||||||||||||||||||||||||||||||||||||||||||||||||||||||||||||||||||||||||||||||||||||||||||||||||||||||||||||||

This top is worked in a combination of knitted and slipped stitches in a very simple pattern composed of colorful horizontal and vertical stripes. If you want to create vertical stripes of colors, use the intarsia technique of working each color with a different ball of yarn and twisting the yarns around each other on the wrong side to prevent holes. For a fun alternative, work the pattern by alternating thick and thin yarns.

FINISHED SIZE
About 31½ (36½, 40)" (80 [92.5, 101.5] cm) bust circumference. Top shown measures 36½" (92.5) cm.

YARN
About 200 grams of a main color (MC) and 50 grams each of five contrasting colors (A, B, C, D and E) of fingering-weight (#1 Super Fine) yarn.

Shown here: **Bomuld** (100% cotton; 228 yd [208 m]/50 g): #15 grass green (MC), 4 skeins; #1 orange (C) and #17 magenta (E), 1 skein each. **Viscolin** (50% viscose, 50% linen; 202 yd [185 m]/50 g): #47 steel gray (A), #43 olive (B), and #40 chartreuse (D), 1 skein each.

NEEDLES
Size U.S. 2 (2.75 mm): straight and 16" (40 cm) circular (cir). Spare needle for three-needle bind-off. Adjust needle size if necessary to obtain the correct gauge.

NOTIONS
Stitch holders; tapestry needle.

GAUGE
27 stitches and 60 rows = 4" (10 cm) in pattern stitch.

NOTE
+ While working neck and armhole shaping, always knit the first and last stitch for selvedges.

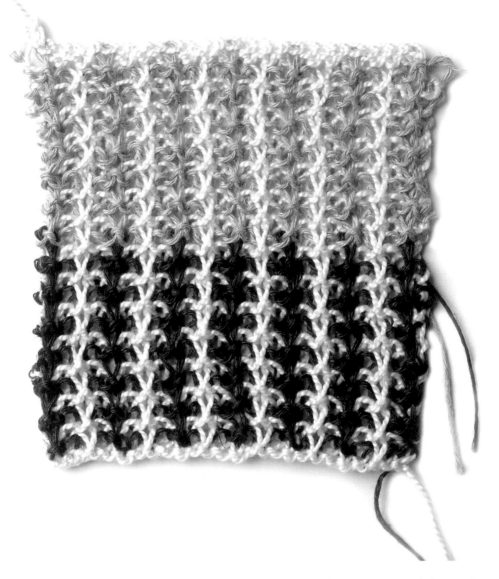

GAUGE SWATCH

NOTE: Swatch shown is worked with white (MC), tan (B), and black (A).

With MC and straight needles, CO 27 sts. Knit 1 row.

ROW 1: (RS) With A, k3, *sl 1 pwise with yarn in back (wyb), k3; rep from *.

ROW 2: (WS) With A, k3, *sl 1 pwise with yarn in front (wyf), k3; rep from *.

ROW 3: With MC, k1, *sl 1 pwise wyb, k3; rep from * to last 2 sts, sl 1 pwise wyb, k1.

ROW 4: With MC, k1, *sl 1 pwise wyf, k3; rep from * to last 2 sts, sl 1 pwise wyf, k1.

Rep Rows 1–4 until a total of 28 rows have been worked. Exchange B for A, then cont in patt until piece measures 2" (5 cm) from color change. BO all sts.

Block as described on page 33.

FRONT

With MC, CO 107 (123, 135) sts. Knit 1 WS row. Rep Rows 1–4 of patt as for gauge swatch, changing contrasting color every 2" (5 cm) as foll: B, C, D, E. Change contrasting color to B and cont in patt with MC and B until piece measures 11 (11½, 13¾)" (28 [29, 35] cm) from CO, ending with a WS row. **NOTE:** For variation, work in desired colors, working top section after stripes with the same color for both MC and B.

Shape Armholes

Knitting the last st of every row, BO 10 sts at beg of next 2 rows, then BO 1 st at the beg of every row 6 (18, 26) times—81 (85, 89) sts rem. Resume knitting the first and last st of every row, work even in patt until armholes measure 2 (2¾, 3½)" (5 [7, 9] cm), ending with a WS row.

Shape Neck

(RS) Cont in patt, work 31 (33, 35) sts, join new yarn and BO next 19 sts, work to end—31 (33, 35) sts rem each side. Working each side separately and knitting the first and last st of every row, at each neck edge BO 7 sts once, then BO 5 sts once, then BO 3 sts once—16 (18, 20) sts rem each side. Dec 1 st at each neck edge every RS row 5 times—11 (13, 15) sts rem. Knitting the first and last st of every row, work even in patt until armholes measure 8 (8¾, 9½)" (20.5 [22, 24] cm), ending with a WS row. Place sts on holders.

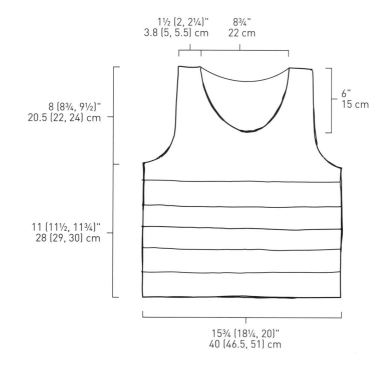

1½ (2, 2¼)"
3.8 (5, 5.5) cm

8¾"
22 cm

8 (8¾, 9½)"
20.5 (22, 24) cm

6"
15 cm

11 (11½, 13¾)"
28 (29, 30) cm

15¾ (18¼, 20)"
40 (46.5, 51) cm

BACK

CO and work as front until armholes measure 4 (4¾, 5½)" (10 [12, 14] cm), ending with a WS row.

Shape Neck

(RS) Cont in patt, work 31 (33, 35) sts, join new yarn and BO next 19 sts, work to end—31 (33, 35) sts rem each side. Work to shoulders as for front neck.

FINISHING

Block to measurements. Place 11 (13, 15) held right front shoulder sts on one needle and 11 (13, 15) corresponding right back shoulder sts on another needle. Holding the front and back with RS facing tog, use the three-needle method (see Glossary) to BO the shoulder sts tog. Rep for other shoulder. With yarn threaded on a tapestry needle, use mattress st (see Glossary) to sew side seams. Weave in loose ends.

Neckband

With MC, cir needle, and RS facing, pick up and knit 196 sts evenly spaced (about 12 sts for every 2" [5 cm]) around neck opening. Join for working in rnds. Work in k2, p2 rib until band measures about 1¼" (3.2 cm) from pick-up rnd. BO all sts. Fold neckband to WS and with yarn threaded on a tapestry needle, sew BO sts to WS along pick-up rnd.

Armbands

With MC, cir needle, and RS facing, pick up and knit 132 sts evenly spaced (about 12 sts for every 2" [5 cm]) around armhole. Work as for neckband.

technique: garment care

||||||||||||||||||||||||||||||||||||||||||||||||||||||||||||||||||||||||||||||||||||||||||||||||||||||||||||||||||||||||||||||||||||||||||||||||

I don't wash wool sweaters very often—it's usually sufficient to hang them outside to air for a few hours. But when washing is necessary, I always do it by hand. I have the best results when I use plenty of cool or lukewarm water and a small amount of quality wool wash or shampoo.

Avoid temperature changes between the wash and rinse water, especially if you're working with wool. If you want to avoid the need for soap, ask your local water department for the pH level of your water. For each 10 liters (quarts) of water add 2 grams (about ½ teaspoon) hexaphosphate per degree of pH to produce a non-alkaline bath, which, when combined with the lanolin from the wool, makes soap and rinsing superfluous.

Wash woolens gently and be careful not to wring them. Gently press the water out of a garment without twisting or wringing it. When I have access to a washing machine with a centrifuge, I put the sweater inside a pillowcase and place it in the spin cycle to remove excess water. Then I lay the sweater on towels to air-dry. In general, wool can hold up to 40% of its weight in water and not feel wet. This is why wool is such a good choice for clothing, especially outdoor wear.

newsprint pullover

The interesting pattern I call "newsprint" is formed by adding a contrast color along with the main color in every third row of knitting. The two colors blend slightly and give an impressionistic look of letters. To create the look of columns of type, the contrasting color is not worked along narrow vertical bands. For added color, a band of diagonal stripes is worked in the intarsia method on the front at the base of the zipper opening.

FINISHED SIZE
About 44¼ (48)" (112.5 [122] cm) chest circumference. Sweater shown measures 48" (122 cm).

YARN
About 250 grams of a main color (MC), 200 grams of a letter color (LC), 50 grams of a contrast color (CC), and 15 grams each of three accent colors (A, B, and C) of fingering-weight (#1 Super Fine) yarn.

Shown here: **Alpaca 2** (50% merino, 50% alpaca; 270 yd [247 m]/50 g): #2105 light gray heather (MC), 5 skeins; #011 steel blue (LC), 4 skeins; #408 medium brown heather (CC), #013 dusty plum (A), #20 teal (B), and #025 coral (C), less than 1 skein each.

NEEDLES
Body and sleeves—size U.S. 4 (3.5 mm): straight and 32" (80 cm) circular (cir). Facings and edgings—size U.S. 2 (3 mm): straight, 16" (40 cm) and two 32" (80 cm) circular (cir). Adjust needle size if necessary to obtain the correct gauge.

NOTIONS
Markers (m); stitch holders; tapestry needle; 8" (20.5 cm) zipper for front neck; sharp-point sewing needle; contrasting sewing thread for basting zipper; matching sewing thread for sewing zipper.

GAUGE
26 stitches and 37 rows = 4" (10 cm) in pattern stitch.

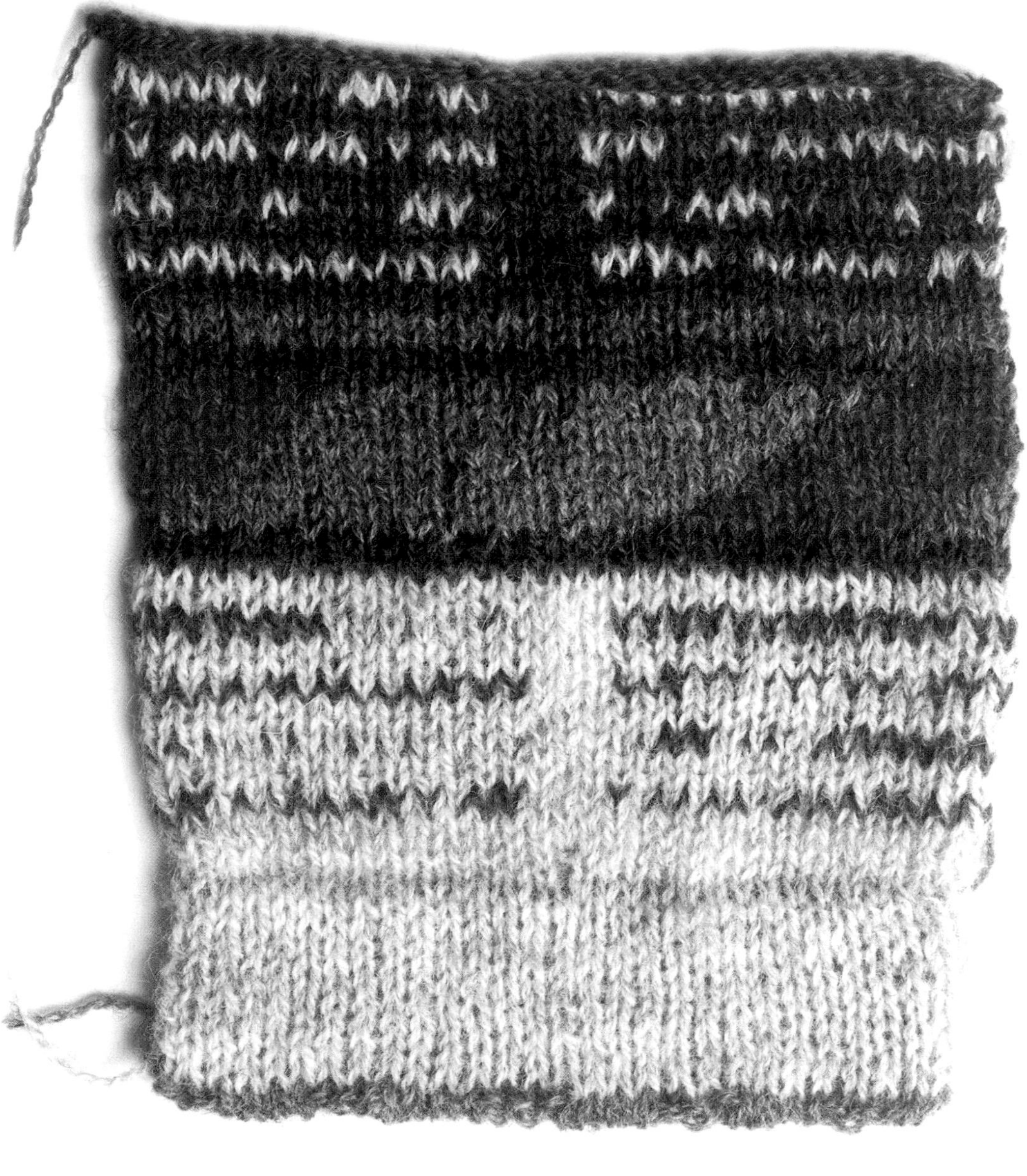

GAUGE SWATCH

With CC and 2 smaller needles held tog, CO 30 sts. Carefully remove 1 needle. Purl 1 WS row.

NEXT ROW: (RS) K1 (edge st), k2, *p3, k3; rep from * to last 3 sts, p2, k1 (edge st).

Knitting the edge sts every row, work in rib as established until piece measures 1½" (3.8 cm) from CO. Cut yarn. Change to MC and larger needles, and work in St st (knit RS rows; purl WS rows) for 1¼" (3.2 cm), ending with a WS row.

With a smaller needle, pick up (do not pick up and knit) 30 sts in the CO row. Hold the needles so that WS face tog and use a third (larger) needle to knit the two sets of sts tog (insert needle into first st on front needle, then the first st on back needle, and knit them together as if they were a single st)—30 sts. Purl 1 WS row.

NEXT ROW: (RS) Knit, using the M1 method (see Glossary) to inc 3 sts evenly spaced—33 sts. (WS).

Purl 1 row. Work newsprint patt as foll.

ROW 1: (RS) K15 with one strand each of MC and LC held tog, k3 with MC only (strand LC loosely across WS), k15 with MC and LC held tog.
ROW 2: (WS) With MC only, k1 (edge st), purl to last st, k1 (edge st).
ROW 3: With MC, knit.
ROW 4: With MC and LC held tog, k1, p14, with MC only (strand LC loosely on WS) p3, with MC and LC held tog, purl to last st, k1.
ROW 5: With MC only, knit.
ROW 6: With MC only, k1, purl to last st, k1.

Rep Rows 1–6 once. With LC, work 2 rows in St st. Cut two 1½-yard (1.4 meter) lengths each of A and B and one 1½-yard (1.4 meter) length of C for the charted intarsia pattern. With RS facing, work the Intarsia chart as foll:

NOTES

+ To prevent the lower edge from drawing in, cast on with two needles held together, then remove one needle before proceeding.

+ The lower body is worked in the round to the armhole, then the front and back are worked separately to the shoulders.

+ The sleeves are worked downward from the armholes to the cuffs.

+ One strand of yarn is used unless otherwise specified.

+ The sweater worn by the model on page 146 is worked with #402 charcoal (MC), #500 black (LC), and three contrasting colors: #025 coral, #016 chartreuse, and #019 light blue.

Intarsia

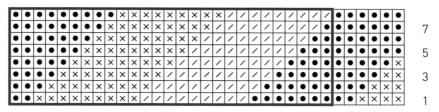

- ⊠ A dusty plum
- ⊡ B teal
- ⊿ C coral
- □ pattern repeat

(RS) K4 with A, k9 with B, k9 with C, k9 with A, k2 with B. Working in the intarsia method (see page 49) of twisting yarns around each other at color changes to prevent holes, work Rows 2–8 of chart, ending with a WS row. Cut off A, B, and C. With LC, work 2 rows in St st, ending with a WS row. With B, work 2 more rows in St st, ending with a WS row. Cut off B. Reversing MC and LC, rep Rows 1–6 of newsprint patt for 1½" (3.8 cm). BO all sts.

Block as described on page 33.

BODY

With CC and two smaller 32" (80 cm) cir needles, CO 258 (282) sts. Place marker (pm) and join for working in rnds, being careful not to twist sts. Remove the second cir needle and proceed with just one. Knit 1 rnd. Work in k3, p3 rib for 2½" (6 cm) for facing. Change to MC and work even in St st for 2" (5 cm). With the other smaller 32" (80 cm) cir needle, pick up 1 st (do not pick up and knit) for every CO loop, hold the needles parallel so that WS of fabric face tog, and use the other end of one smaller 32" (80 cm) cir needle to knit the sts from the other two needles tog—still 258 (282) sts. Knit 1 rnd, inc 30 sts evenly spaced—288 (312) sts. Change to larger 32" (80 cm) cir needle and MC and LC. Work newsprint patt as foll.

RND 1: (RS) *K21 (23) with MC and LC held tog, k3 with MC alone (strand LC loosely across WS); rep from * to end.

RNDS 2 AND 3: With MC only, knit.

Rep Rnd 1–3, until piece measures 15¾" (40 cm) from start of newsprint patt, ending with Rnd 2.

DIVIDE FOR FRONT AND BACK

Place markers at each side, just after a column of 3 MC sts. With RS facing and keeping in patt, *work to 14 (15) sts before first marked side seam st, BO next 25 (27) sts for underarm; rep from * once more —119 (129) sts rem each for front and back.

Place back sts on holder to work later.

FRONT

Working back and forth on 119 (129) front sts, work 2 rows in St st with LC, ending with a WS row. Work Rows 1–8 of Intarsia chart, alternating 9 sts each of A, B, and C. With LC, work 2 rows in St st. With B, work 2 rows in St st. With LC, work 2 rows in St st.

Front Neck Split

ROW 1: (RS) K1 with LC alone, k9 (10) with MC and LC held tog, [k3 with LC alone (strand MC loosely across WS) k21 (23) with both colors] 2 times, k1 with LC alone, join a second ball of LC and BO 1 st, k1 with LC alone, join a second ball of MC, [k21 (23) with both colors, k3 with LC alone (strand MC loosely across WS)] 2 times, k9 (10) with both colors, k1 with LC alone—59 (64) sts rem on each side.

Cont working each side separately as foll.

ROW 2: (WS) With LC only, k1 (edge st), purl to 1 st before neck split, k1 (edge st); on other side: With LC only, k1 (edge st), purl to last st, k1 (edge st).

ROW 3: With LC, knit.

ROW 4: K1 with LC only, p9 (11) with MC and LC held tog, [p3 with LC alone (strand MC loosely across WS), p21 (23) with both colors] 2 times, k1 with LC alone; on other side: k1 with LC only, [p21 (23) with both colors, p3 with LC alone (strand MC loosely across WS)] 2 times, p9 (10) with both colors, k1 with LC alone.

ROW 5: With LC only, knit.

ROW 6: With LC only, k1 (edge st), purl to 1 st before neck split, k1 (edge st); on other side: With LC only, k1 (edge st), purl to last st, k1 (edge st).

Cont in patt until front split measures 6" (15 cm).

Shape Front Neck

Keeping in patt, at each neck edge, BO 5 sts once, then BO 4 sts once, then BO 3 sts 2 times, then BO 2 sts 2 times, then BO 1 st 4 times, ending with a WS row—36 (41) sts rem. Change to CC and St st and *at the same time* BO 1 st at each neck edge 2 more times—34 (39) sts rem.

NEXT ROW: (RS) Work across, BO 1 st at one neck edge.

NEXT ROW: (WS) Work across, BO 1 st at other neck edge—33 (38) sts rem each side for shoulders.

Place these sts on holders.

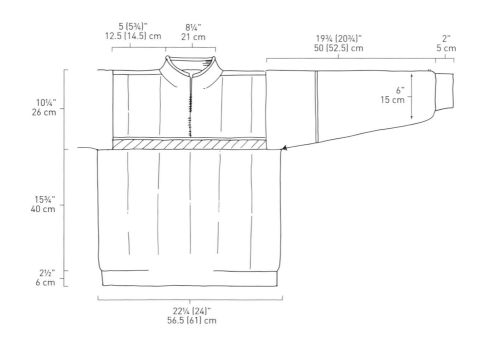

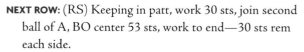

BACK

Return 119 (129) held back sts to needle.

ROW 1: (RS) K1 with LC only, k9 (10) with MC and LC held tog, [k3 with LC only (strand MC loosely across WS) k21 (23) with both colors] 4 times, k3 with only (strand MC loosely across WS), k9 (10) with both colors, k1 with LC only.

ROW 2: (WS) With LC only, k1 (edge st), purl to last st, k1 (edge st).

ROW 3: With LC, knit.

ROW 4: K1 with LC only, p9 (11) with MC and LC held tog, [p3 with LC only, p21 (23) with both colors] 4 times, p3 with LC only, p9 (10) with both colors, k1 with LC only.

ROW 5: With LC only, knit.

ROW 6: With LC only, k1 (edge st), purl to last st, k1 (edge st).

Cont in patt until piece measures same as front to color change, ending with 1 row of LC. Change to CC and St st and work 6 rows even. Change to MC and work 1 row. Place sts on holder.

JOIN FRONT AND BACK AT SHOULDERS

Place 33 (38) held right front shoulder sts on one needle and 33 (38) corresponding right back shoulder sts on another needle. Hold the pieces with RS facing tog and use the three-needle method (see Glossary) to BO the shoulder sts tog. Rep for other shoulder—53 sts rem for back neck.

Neckband

With LC and RS facing, pick up and knit 30 sts along right front neck, work across 53 back neck sts from holder, pick up and knit 30 sts along left front neck—113 sts total. Knitting the first and last st of every row, work in St st for 1½" (3.8 cm). Knit 1 WS row for turning ridge. Change to A and work in St st, knitting the first and last st of every row for 2" (5 cm), ending with a WS row.

NEXT ROW: (RS) Keeping in patt, work 30 sts, join second ball of A, BO center 53 sts, work to end—30 sts rem each side.

NEXT ROW: (WS) K1, purl to neck edge, use the backward-loop method (see Glossary) to CO 5 sts; on other side: purl to last st, k1.

Work short-rows (see page 72) as foll.

SHORT-ROW 1: (RS) Knit to neck edge, use the backward-loop method to CO 5 sts; on other side: k6, wrap next st, turn work.

SHORT-ROW 2: (WS) Purl to 1 st before neck edge, k1; on other side: k1, p6 (hide the wrap by knitting it tog with the wrapped st), wrap next st, turn.

SHORT-ROW 3: K4, ssk, k1; on other side, k1, k2tog, k4 (hiding the wrap as before), wrap next st, turn—1 st dec'd each side.

SHORT-ROWS 4–16: Rep Short-rows 2 and 3 six times, then rep Short-row 2 once more—28 sts rem each side.

SHORT-ROW 17: K4, ssk, k1; on other side, k1, k2tog, k5 (hiding wrap), wrap next st, turn—27 sts rem each side.

SHORT-ROW 18: Purl to 1 st before neck edge, k1; on other side, k1, p7 (hiding wrap), wrap next st, turn.

SHORT-ROW 19: K5, ssk, k1; on other side, k1, k2tog, k6 (hiding wrap), wrap next st, turn—26 sts rem each side.

SHORT-ROW 20: Purl to 1 st before neck edge, k1; on other side, k1, p8 (hiding wrap), wrap next st, turn.

SHORT-ROW 21: K6, ssk, k1; on other side, k1, k2tog, k8 (hiding wrap), wrap next st, turn—25 sts rem each side.

SHORT-ROW 22: Purl to 1 st before neck edge, k1; on other side, k1, p10 (hiding wrap), wrap next st, turn.

SHORT-ROW 23: K8, ssk, k1; on other side, k1, k2tog, k10 (hiding wrap), wrap next st, turn—24 sts rem each side.

SHORT-ROW 24: Purl to 1 st before neck edge, k1; on other side, k1, p12 (hiding wrap), wrap next st, turn.

SHORT-ROW 25: K10, ssk, k1; on other side, k1, k2tog, k13 (hiding wrap), wrap next st, turn—23 sts rem each side.

SHORT-ROW 26: Purl to 1 st before neck edge, k1; on other side, k1, p15 (hiding wrap), wrap next st, turn.

ROW 27: Knit to 3 sts before neck edge, ssk, k1; on other side, k1, k2tog, knit to end, hiding wrap when you come to it—1 st dec'd each side; 22 sts rem each side).

ROW 28: K1, purl to 1 st before neck edge, k1; on other side, k1, purl to last st, hiding the wrap when you come to it, k1.

ROWS 29–52: Rep the last 2 rows 12 times—10 sts rem each side.

ROW 53: Knit.

ROW 54: K1, purl to 1 st before neck edge, k1; on other side, k1, purl to last st, k1.

Rep the last 2 rows until facing measures ¾" (2 cm) longer than zipper opening. BO all sts.

SLEEVES

With LC, larger needles, and beg and end at underarm, pick up and knit 131 sts evenly spaced around armhole.

ROW 1: (WS) K1 with LC only, p27 (24) with MC and LC held tog, [p3 with LC only (strand MC loosely across WS), p21 (23) with both colors] 3 times, p3 with LC only (strand MC loosely across WS), p27 (24) with MC and LC, k1 with LC only.

ROW 2: (RS) With LC only, knit.

ROW 3: With LC only, k1 (edge st), purl to last st, k1 (edge st).

ROW 4: K1 with LC only, k27 (24) with both colors, [k3 with LC only, k21 (23) with both colors] 3 times, k3 with LC only, k27 (24) with both colors, k1 with LC only.

ROW 5: With LC only, k1 (edge st), purl to last st, k1 (edge st).

ROW 6: With LC only, knit.

Cont in patt until piece measures 2" (5 cm) from pick-up row, ending with a WS row.

DEC ROW: (RS) K1, ssk, work in patt to last 3 sts, k2tog, k1—2 sts dec'd.

Dec 1 st each end of needle in this manner every 6th row 26 more times and *at the same time*, after 6" (15 cm), work 2 rows in St st with LC, then 2 rows in St st with B, then work newsprint patt reversing colors—77 sts rem when all shaping has been completed. Work even in patt until piece measures 19¾ (20¾)" (50 [52.5] cm) from pick-up row, or 2" (5 cm) less than desired total length, ending with a WS row of MC only.

DEC ROW: (RS) Knit, dec 11 sts evenly spaced—66 sts rem.

Change to smaller needle and with MC, work in St st for 2" (5 cm). Change to B. Work in k3, p3 rib for 2½" (6.5 cm) for facing. BO all sts. Work the other sleeve to match, but work the facing with C.

FINISHING

Weave in loose ends. Carefully steam-press garment on WS. With yarn threaded on a tapestry needle, use the mattress st (see Glossary) to sew sleeve seams. Sew sleeve facing (BO edge) to WS of sleeve, allowing a small band of facing color to show on RS. Sew zipper to WS of front opening (see Glossary), allowing extra length of zipper to extend on WS below slit if necessary. Sew facing along zipper opening and back neck. Neatly join the last ¾" (2 cm) of the front facings below the zipper. The 5 facing sts that were CO when binding off for the back neck should be sewn down along the WS of the shoulder. Steam-press all seams.

technique: stranded two-color knitting

||||||||||||||||||||||||||||||||||||||||||||||||||||||||||||||||||||||||||||||||||||||||||||||||||||||||||||||||||||||||||||||||

STRANDED TWO-COLOR KNITTING

Stranded two-color knitting, also called jacquard or Fair Isle knitting, involves working with two colors at the same time, although in such a way that one color is stranded across the back (wrong side) of the work while the other color is being knitted. The keys to success are even tension (the unworked strands must have the same widthwise tension as the knitting) and consistent use of the two colors so that one color is the dominant color throughout.

Dominant Color

The manner in which you hold the two yarns in stranded knitting may result in the stitches of one color being slightly larger than the stitches of the other, causing them to "pop" out from the background on the right side of the work. The slightly more prominent stitches are said to be in the dominant color.

For best results, use the Continental method of knitting and hold both yarns in your left hand. Hold one color over your index finger and the other over both your index and middle fingers (Figure 1). It is worthwhile to learn this method as it offers several advantages:

+ The two strands are not in contact with each other and therefore cannot tangle.

+ The strand that is not worked (the "float") will have the same tension as the strand that is knitted, therefore the fabric is less likely to pucker.

+ The strand that lies closest to the knitting (the one that lies over just your index finger) will be the primary strand in the pattern. The stitches made with this strand will be slightly larger than the others and, therefore, this strand is designated the dominant color.

To practice, you will need needles and two colors of yarn—one light and one dark. Cast on 8 stitches with the light yarn. Place the yarns over the index and middle fingers of your left hand as shown in Figure 1 so that the light yarn is in the dominant position—farthest from your finger tip and draped over just your index finger. Alternate one stitch of each color in stockinette stitch as follows:

Right-Side Rows

STEP 1: Knit the first stitch with both colors held together.

STEP 2: Insert the right needle through the second stitch and knit it with the light yarn (Figure 2).

STEP 3: Insert the right needle through the next stitch, bring it over the light yarn, and knit the stitch with the dark yarn (Figure 3).

Alternate Steps 2 and 3 (working one stitch each of each color) in this manner to the last stitch. Knit the last stitch with both colors held together (Figure 4).

Wrong-Side Rows

To keep the light yarn dominant on the right side of the piece while working wrong-side rows, rearrange the yarns in your left hand so that the dark yarn is positioned as the dominant color—so that the dark color is farthest from your fingertips and is draped over just your index finger.

STEP 1: Knit the first stitch with both colors held together.

STEP 2: Insert the needle under both yarns, then purl the next stitch with the dark yarn (Figure 5), pulling the stitch under the light yarn so that the light yarn remains on the wrong side of the work (Figure 6).

STEP 3: Insert the needle under both yarns, purl the next stitch with the light yarn, catching the light yarn over the top of the dark yarn and pulling the stitch under the dark yarn so that the dark yarn remains on the wrong side of the work (Figure 7).

Alternate Steps 2 and 3 to the last stitch. Knit the last stitch with both colors held together (Figure 8).

To work stranded two-color knitting in rounds, the right side of the work will always face you and there will be no edge stitches. Therefore, you will always hold the two yarns the same way and will work every stitch with just one color.

Figure 1

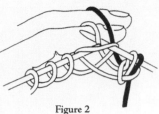

Figure 2

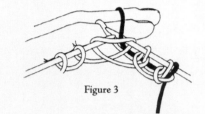

Figure 3

Figure 4

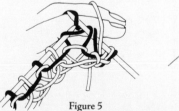

Figure 5

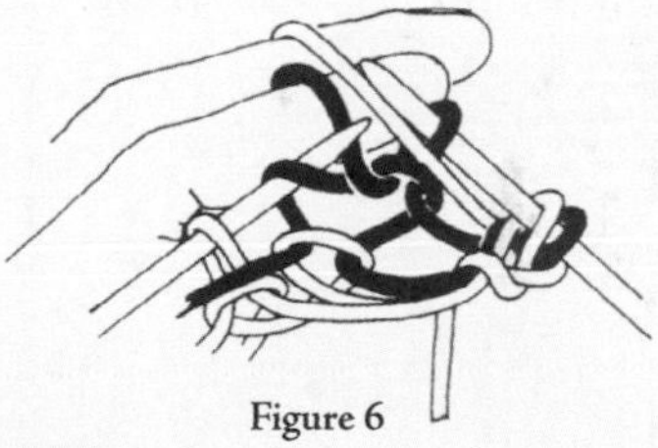

Figure 6

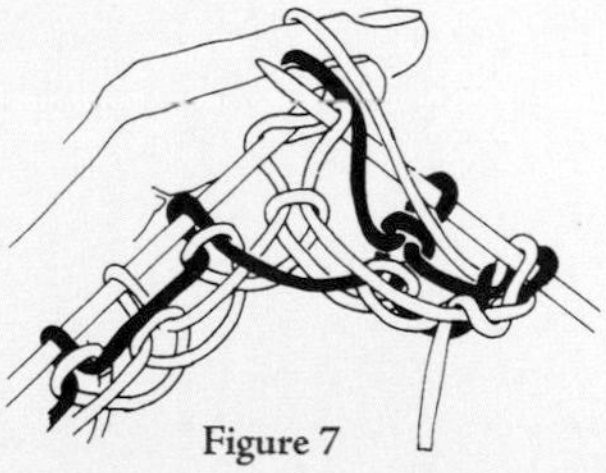

Figure 7

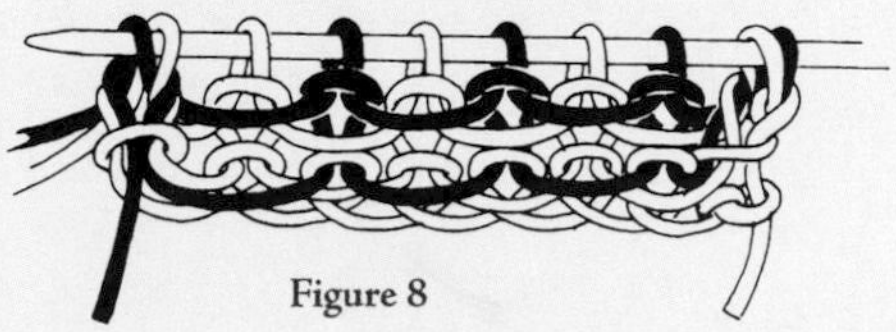

Figure 8

newsprint top

|||||||||||||||||||||||||||||||||||||||||||||||||||||||||||||||||||||||||||||||||||||||||||||||||||||||||||||||||||||||||||||||||||||||||||||||||||||||

This short-sleeve sweater is worked in two halves, each beginning at a side "seam." Both halves are worked in stripes that form an overall chevron pattern worked in stripes of garter stitch and stockinette stitch that features the same newsprint pattern as the Newsprint Pullover on page 146. This design lends itself well to exciting variations. Try working stripes in various combinations of stockinette and garter stitch in various color combinations for a completely different look.

FINISHED SIZE
About 37¼ (40¼)" (94.5 [102] cm) bust circumference. Top shown measures 37¼" (94.5 cm).

YARN
About 200 (250) grams of a main color (MC) of fingering-weight (#1 Super Fine) yarn and about 50 grams of a contrasting color (CC) of fingering-weight yarn.

Shown here: **Bomuld** (100% cotton; 228 yd [208 m]/50 g): #0 natural (MC), 4 (5) skeins. **Viscolin** (50% viscose, 50% linen; 202 yd [185 m]/50 g): #47 steel gray (CC), 1 skein.

NEEDLES
Size U.S. 2 (3 mm): straight and 24" (60 cm) circular (cir). Adjust needle size if necessary to obtain the correct gauge.

NOTIONS
Stitch markers; stitch holders; tapestry needle.

GAUGE
24 stitches and 31 rows in chevron pattern as established in gauge swatch= 4" (10 cm).

NOTES
+ Work with two strands of CC held together for the contrast color.

+ It is important to get the correct row gauge for this top.

+ The top is worked in two halves, each beginning at the lower side "seam."

+ The gauge swatch can be used for the beginning of the sweater.

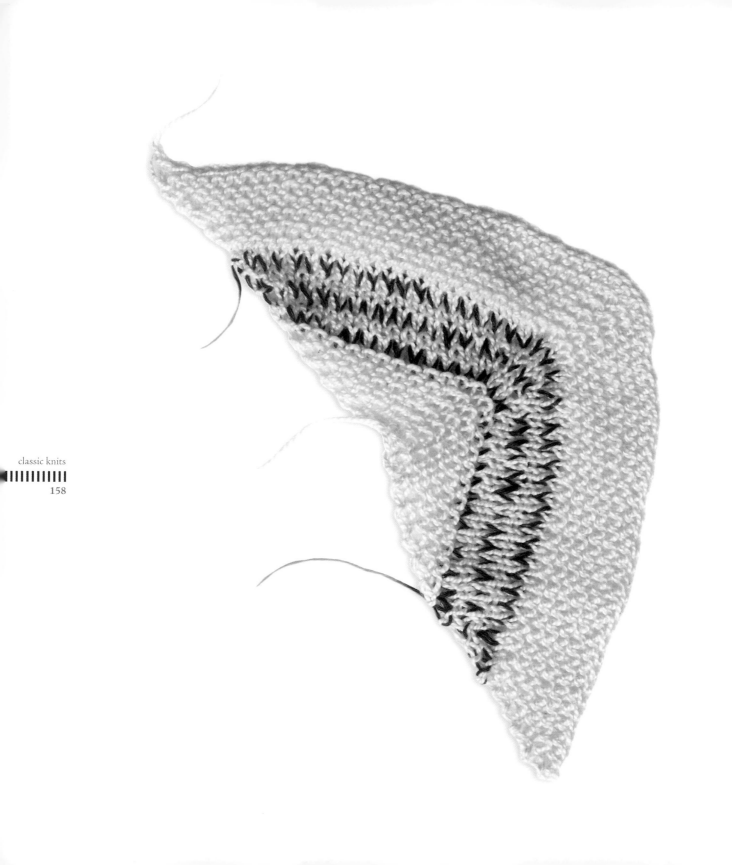

GAUGE SWATCH

With MC, CO 4 sts.

ROW 1: (RS) K1, M1 (see Glossary), place marker (pm), k2, pm, M1, k1—6 sts.

ROWS 2, 4, 6, 8, AND 10: (WS) Knit.

ROW 3: [K1, M1] 2 times, slip marker (sl m), k2, sl m, [M1, k1] 2 times—10 sts.

ROWS 5, 7, 9, AND 11: K1, M1, knit to m , M1, sl m, k2, sl m, M1, knit to last st, M1, k1—4 sts inc'd; 26 sts after Row 11.

ROW 12: Knit.

Size 40¼" Only

ROW 13: K1, M1, knit to m , M1, sl m, k2, sl m, M1, knit to last st, M1, k1—30 sts.

ROW 14: Knit.

Both Sizes

ROWS 13, 15, 17, AND 19 (15, 17, 19, 21, AND 23): With CC, k1, M1, knit to m, M1, sl m, k2, sl m, M1, knit to last st, M1, k1—4 sts inc'd; 42 (50) sts after Row 19 (23).

ROWS 14, 16 19, AND 20 (16, 19, 20, 22, AND 24): With MC, k1, purl to last st, k1.

These 20 (24) rows set up the patt for the sweater. Rep Rows 11 and 12 six (seven) more times to make it easier to measure the gauge. Place the sts on a holder.

Block as described on page 33.

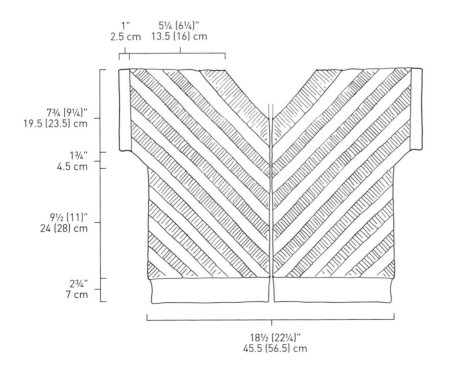

1"
2.5 cm

5¼ (6¼)"
13.5 (16) cm

7¾ (9¼)"
19.5 (23.5) cm

1¾"
4.5 cm

9½ (11)"
24 (28) cm

2¾"
7 cm

18½ (22¼)"
45.5 (56.5) cm

HALF OF BODY (MAKE 2)

With MC, CO 4 sts. Work Rows 1–20 (24) as for gauge swatch—42 (50 sts). *Rep Rows 11 and 12 six (seven) times—66 (78) sts. Work Rows 13–20 (15–24)—82 (98) sts. Rep from * 1 more time—122 (146) sts. Rep Rows 11 and 12 six (seven) times—146 (174) sts; piece measures 9¼ (11)" (23.5 [28] cm) from CO to point of triangle.

Shape Armhole

Working Row 13 (15) of patt, work to m, M1, sl m, k1, use the backward-loop method (see Glossary) to CO 10 sts, join a second ball of each CC, CO 10 more sts, work to end in patt—85 (99) sts each side. Working each side separately, work Rows 14–20 (16–24) of patt—91 (107) sts each side. Do not cut yarns. Place sts on holder.

Make another piece to match.

Back

With RS facing, slip all sts to cir needle, removing markers—364 (428) sts total. Arrange sts to begin at an armhole edge (the center of one half). Work back and forth on 182 (214) back sts only as foll.

ROW 1: (RS) Work across the second set of sts on the first half of sweater as foll: With MC, k1, M1, knit to 3 sts before end of this half, ssk, pm, k1; with same ball of yarn, work across the first set of sts on the second half of sweater as foll: k1, pm, k2tog, knit to last st, M1, k1, turn.

ROWS 2, 4, 6, 8, 10, AND 12: Knit.

ROWS 3, 5, 7, 9, AND 11: With MC, k1, M1, knit to 2 sts before m, ssk, sl m, k2, sl m, k2tog, knit to last st, M1, k1.

Size 40¼" Only

ROW 13: Rep Row 3.

ROW 14: Rep Row 2.

Both Sizes

ROWS 13, 15, 17, AND 19 (15, 17, 19, 21, AND 23): With CC, k1, M1, knit to 2 sts before m, ssk, sl m, k2, sl m, k2tog, knit to last st, M1, k1.

ROW 14, 16, 18, AND 20 (16, 18, 20, 22, AND 24): With MC, k1, purl to last st, k1.

ROWS 21, 23, 25, 27, 29, AND 31 (25, 27, 29, 31, 33, 35, AND 37): Rep Row 3.

ROWS 22, 24, 26, 28, 30, AND 32 (26, 28, 30, 32, 34, 36, AND 38): Rep Row 2.

Rep Rows 13–32 (15–38) once more—piece measures about 17 (20¼)" (43 [51.5] cm) from CO. Place sts on holder.

Front

Work across the rem 91 (107) sts on cir needle back and forth in rows as for back. Keep sts on needle.

With RS facing, slip back sts onto cir needle with front sts—364 (428) sts total.

Shoulders

Begin working in the round on both back and front sts as foll.

RND 1: With CC, *k1, pm, k2tog, knit to 2 sts before next m, ssk, sl m, k2, sl m, k2tog, knit to 3 sts before end of this piece, ssk, pm, k1; with same ball of yarn, rep from * once—8 sts dec'd; 356 (420) sts rem.

RNDS 2, 4, 6, AND 8: With MC, knit.

RNDS 3, 5, AND 7: With CC, *k1, sl m, k2tog, knit to 2 sts before next m, ssk, sl m, k2, sl m, k2tog, knit to 2 sts before next m, ssk, sl m, k1; rep from * once more—8 sts dec'd; 322 (396) sts rem after Rnd 7.

Size 44¼" Only

RND 9: Rep Rnd 3—388 sts rem.

RND 10: Rep Rnd 2.

Both Sizes

RNDS 9, 11, 13, 15, 17, AND 19 (11, 13, 15, 17, 19, 21, AND 23): With MC, *k1, sl m, k2tog, knit to 2 sts before next marker, ssk, sl m, k2, sl m, k2tog, knit to 2 sts before next m, ssk, sl m, k1; rep from * once more—8 sts dec'd; 284 (332) sts rem after Rnd 19 (23).

RNDS 10, 12, 14, 16, 18, AND 20 (12, 14, 16, 18, 20, 22, AND 24): With MC, purl.

Rep Rnd 3—276 (324) sts rem.
Rep Rnds 2–8 (2–10)—252 (292) sts rem.
Rep Rnds 9–20 (11–24)—204 (236) sts rem.
BO all sts knitwise.

FINISHING

Sleeve Edging

With MC, straight needle, RS facing, and beg at underarm, pick up and knit about 81 (97) sts around sleeve edge. Work in garter st for 12 (16) rows, ending with a WS row—6 (8) garter ridges. With RS facing, BO all sts knitwise. With yarn threaded on a tapestry needle, sew the armhole CO sts and edging tog at the underarm.

Lower Edge

With MC, cir needle, and RS facing, pick up and knit about 288 (344) sts evenly around lower edge. Work in garter st until edging measures 2¾" (7 cm) from pick-up row. BO all sts.

Block to measurements. Weave in loose ends.

black and white

The bold geometric patterns in this sweater were inspired by traditional African motifs. I worked the zigzags in the tweed "newsprint" technique used for the garments on pages 146 and 156 that I positioned against large blocks of black and white. This pattern looks good on both sides of the fabric—with the zigzags worked in stockinette stitch against a reverse stockinette-stitch background (as shown here) or with the zigzags worked in reverse stockinette stitch against a stockinette-stitch background. Decide which you prefer after knitting the gauge swatch, then be sure to strand the unused yarn across the wrong side of the garment accordingly.

FINISHED SIZE
About 38½ (45)" (98 [114.5] cm) bust circumference. Sweater shown measures 38½" (98 cm).

YARN
About 150 (200) grams each of a light color (L1) and a dark color (D1) of laceweight (#0 Lace) yarn, 150 (200) grams each of a light color (L2) and a dark color (D2) of a different laceweight yarn, and 50 grams of a contrasting color (CC) of laceweight yarn.

Shown here: **Alpaca 1** (100% alpaca; 437 yd [400 m]/50 g): #100 natural (L1) and #500 black (D1), 3 (4) skeins each. **Wool 1** (100% wool; 340 yd [311 m]/50 g): #2s light gray heather (L2) and #47 steel gray (D2), 3 (4) skeins each; #1 chartreuse (CC), 1 skein.

NEEDLES
Size U.S. 4 (3.5 mm): 24" and 16" (60 and 40 cm) circular (cir) and spare needle for 3-needle bind-off. Adjust needle size if necessary to obtain the correct gauge.

NOTIONS
Tapestry needle.

GAUGE
22 stitches and 30 rows = 4" (10 cm) in charted pattern with two strands of yarn held together for the solid-color sections and three strands of yarn held together for the tweed zigzag section.

GAUGE SWATCH

With short cir needle and one strand each of D1 and D2 held tog, CO 24 sts. Knit 5 rows, ending with a WS row.

NEXT ROW: (RS) K2, p1, *k3, p3; rep from * to last 3 sts, k3.

NEXT ROW: (WS) K1, sl 1 with yarn in front (wyf), p1, *k3, p3; rep from * to last 3 sts, k1, sl 1 wyf, k1.

Rep the last 2 rows until piece measures 1¼" (3.2 cm) from CO, ending with a WS row. Change to one strand each of L1 and L2 held tog and work chart patt as foll: Working first 2 and last 2 sts as established, follow 21 rows of Swatch chart, working tweed zigzag color patt with one strand of D2 held tog with one strand each of L1 and L2 (three strands total), leaving D2 on the WS when not in use. Cut yarn and slide sts to other end of needle. Rejoin yarn to beg of RS row. With RS facing, work horizontal chain st (see page 169) for 1 row. Purl 1 WS row. With RS facing, BO all sts.

Block swatch as described on page 33.

FRONT

With long cir needle and one strand each of D1 and D2 held tog, CO 36 (42) sts, then with one strand each of L1 and L2 held tog, CO 36 (42) more sts, then with another ball each of D1 and D2 held tog, CO 36 (42) more sts— 108 (126) sts total. Keeping colors as established, twisting yarns around each other at color changes (see Notes), knit 5 rows.

NEXT ROW: (WS) K1, sl 1 with yarn in front (wyf), p1, *k3, p3; rep from * to last 3 sts, k1, sl 1 wyf, k1.

NEXT ROW: (RS) K2, p1, *k3, p3; rep from * to last 3 sts, k3. Rep the last 2 rows until ribbed section measures 4" (10 cm). Reversing colors so that light is over dark and dark is over light, work Rows 1–57 of Block chart in each color section, working first 2 and last 2 sts as established. Break yarn and slide sts to other end of needle. Rejoin yarn to beg of RS row.

NOTES

+ Work with two strands of yarn held together (L1 and L2 or D1 and D2) for the background blocks; work with three strands of yarn (both light plus one dark or both dark plus one light) held together for the tweed zigzag pattern.

+ Work color blocks in the intarsia method (see page 49) of using separate balls or bobbins of yarn for each block and twisting the yarns around each other at color changes to prevent holes.

+ Work the blocks checkerboard fashion so that light is over dark and vice versa.

+ Begin and end each right-side row with k2; beg each wrong-side row with k1, sl 1 with yarn in front (wyf) and end each wrong-side row with sl 1 wyf, k1.

+ Slip stitches purlwise with yarn in front on wrong-side rows.

+ Each block is 36 (42) sts wide and 57 rows tall.

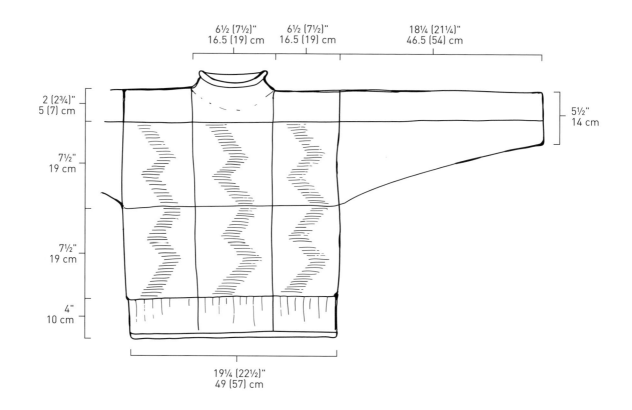

6½ (7½)"
16.5 (19) cm

6½ (7½)"
16.5 (19) cm

18¼ (21¼)"
46.5 (54) cm

2 (2¾)"
5 (7) cm

5½"
14 cm

7½"
19 cm

7½"
19 cm

4"
10 cm

19¼ (22½)"
49 (57) cm

NEXT ROW: (RS) Work horizontal chain stitch (see page 169).

Break yarn and slide sts to other end of needle. Rejoin to beg of RS row and work Rows 57–1 of Block chart again, reversing colors and reversing zigzags by working the chart from the top down. Break yarn and slide sts to other end of needle. Rejoin yarn to beg of RS row. Work horizontal chain stitch. Break yarn and slide sts to other end of needle. Rejoin yarn to beg of RS row and reverse colors. Work even in rev St st in colors as established (i.e., do not work zigzag patt) until piece measures ¾" (2 cm) from last horizontal chain.

Shape Neck

Keeping in color patt, work 49 (58) sts, join new yarn and BO the center 10 sts, work to end—49 (58) sts rem each side. Working each side separately, at each neck edge, BO 4 sts once, then BO 3 sts once, then BO 2 sts 3 times, then

BO 1 st 0 (3) times—36 (42) sts rem each side. Work even until piece measures 2¾ (3½)" (7 [9] cm) from last horizontal chain. Place sts on holders.

BACK

Work as for front but reverse the colors and omit the neckline shaping until piece measures same as front to shoulders.

JOIN FRONT TO BACK AT SHOULDERS

Place 36 (42) held right front shoulder sts on one needle. Hold the front and back pieces with RS facing tog and use the three-needle bind-off method (see Glossary) to BO the 36 (42) shoulder sts tog. Place the next 36 (42) sts from back on a holder for back neck. Rep three-needle bind-off for other shoulder.

Block

Swatch

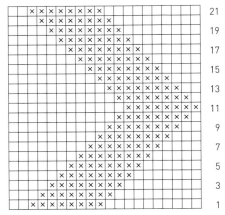

57
55
53
51
49
47
45
43
41
39
37
35
33
31
29
27
25
23
21
19
17
15
13
11
9
7
5
3
1

21
19
17
15
13
11
9
7
5
3
1

☐ background color

☒ pattern color

↑ begin medium ↑ begin large

SLEEVES

With RS facing, using light yarn along the dark blocks and dark yarn along the light blocks, and beg and ending at the color change between the two rows of zigzag blocks, pick up and knit 106 (114) sts evenly spaced (about 11 sts for every 2" [5 cm]) around selvedge edge of front and back. Working the first and last 2 sts as for body, work back and forth in intarsia in rev St st for 4 more rows.

DEC ROW: (WS) Work the 2 edge sts as established, k2tog, work to last 4 sts, k2tog, work the 2 edge sts as established—2 sts dec'd.

Dec 1 st each end of needle in this manner every 6th row 22 (26) more times—60 sts rem. Work even until sleeve measures 18¼ (21¼)" (46.5 [54] cm) from pick-up row. With two strands of CC held tog, knit 2 rows.

Trim

With previously established dark and light colors, work in rev St st for 1¼" (3 cm). BO all sts.

FINISHING

Neckband

Place 36 (42) held back neck sts on short cir needle. Maintaining colors as established, pick up and knit about 50 sts around front neck—86 (92) sts total. Working back and forth in rows, work rev St st until neckband measures about 2" (5 cm) from pick-up row, or desired length. Knit 2 rows for turning ridge, then cont in rev St st for facing until facing measures same length as neckband. BO all sts. Fold neckband to WS along turning ridge and, with yarn threaded on a tapestry needle, sew to WS. With two strands of CC held tog and RS facing, pick up and knit 1 st in each loop of the turning ridge of neckband. Work in St st for 6 rows. BO all sts. Allow edge to roll forward.

Weave in loose ends. Block to measurements. With yarn threaded on a tapestry needle, use the mattress st (see Glossary) to sew sleeve and side seams. Sew facings to WS. Carefully steam-press all seams.

technique: horizontal chain stitch

||||||||||||||||||||||||||||||||||||||||||||||||||||||||||||||||||||||||||||||||||||||||||||||||||||||||||||||

With the right side facing, knit the edge stitch, then increase one stitch by working into the front of back of the next stitch (Figure 1). Return the last stitch worked (shown in black) back onto the left needle (Figure 2). *Skip this stitch and knit through the back loop of the next stitch (Figure 3). Knit the skipped stitch and return it to the left needle (Figure 4). This stitch now lies horizontally across the knitted fabric.

Repeat from * to the last two stitches, then knit the last two stitches together to return to the original stitch count. Work the next row as usual—the stitches in this row will appear elongated and form a bit of an eyelet texture (Figure 5); to tighten up the stitches, work them through their back loops.

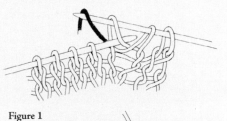

Figure 1

Figure 2

Figure 3

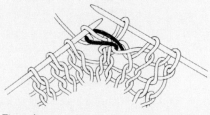

Figure 4

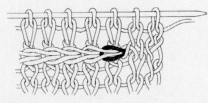

Figure 5

relief

I designed this textured pullover many years ago, but I still enjoy how the ribs curve around the seed-stitch blocks. The design works well in a thick yarn, which makes the relief structure pop. Accents of a contrasting color punctuate the edgings and the boundary between the ribbing and body pattern. This pattern makes a thick and warm sweater.

FINISHED SIZE
About 30¾ (35½, 40)" (78 [90, 101.5] cm) chest circumference. To fit 3 (7, 11) years. Sweater shown measures 35½" (90 cm).

YARN
About 200 (250, 300) grams of a main color (MC1) of fingering-weight (#1 Super Fine) yarn. About 150 (200, 200) grams of a second main color (MC2) and 200 (250, 300) grams of a third main color (MC3), and 50 grams of a contrast color (CC) of laceweight (#0 Lace) yarn.

Shown here: **Alpaca 2** (50% merino, 50% alpaca; 270 yd [247 m]/50 g): #2105 light gray heather (MC1), 4 (5, 6) skeins. **Alpaca 1** (100% alpaca; 437 yd [400 m]/50 g): #402 charcoal (MC2), 3 (4, 4) skeins. **Wool 1** (100% wool; 340 yd [311 m]/50 g): #0 natural (MC3), 4 (5, 6) skeins; #28s coral (CC), 1 (1, 1) skein.

NEEDLES
Size U.S. 4 (3.5 mm): straight and 16" (40 cm) circular (cir). Adjust needle size if necessary to obtain the correct gauge.

NOTIONS
Stitch holders; removable markers; tapestry needle.

GAUGE
21 stitches and 28 rows = 4" (10 cm) in stitch pattern with one strand each of MC1, MC2, and MC3 held together.

NOTE
+ Work with one strand each of MC1, MC2, and MC3 held together (three strands total for the main color); work the contrasting color with two strands of CC held together for the constrasting color.

GAUGE SWATCH

With two strands of CC held tog and straight needles, CO 21 sts. Change to one strand each of MC1, MC2, and MC3 held tog. Work Relief chart as foll.

ROW 1: (WS) *K1, p1; rep from * to last st, k1.

ROW 2: K1, [k1, p1] 3 times, *k1 [k1, p1] 2 times, k1, [k1, p1] 3 times; rep from * to last 2 sts, k2.

ROWS 3–8: Rep Rows 1 and 2 three times.

ROW 9: Rep Row 1.

ROW 10: K2, [k1, p1] 2 times, *k1, [k1, p1] 3 times, k1, [k1, p1] 2 times; rep from * to last 3 sts, k3.

ROWS 11–17: Rep Rows 3 and 4 three times, then work Row 1 once more.

ROW 18: (RS) With two strands of CC held tog, k1, sl 1 with yarn in back (wyb), k5, *[sl 1 wyb, p1] 3 times, sl 1 wyb, k5; rep from * to last 2 sts, sl 1 wyb, k1.

ROW 19: (WS) With CC, k1, sl 1 with yarn in front (wyf), k5 *[sl 1 wyf, p1] 3 times, sl 1 wyf, k5; rep from * to last 2 sts, sl 1 wyf, k1.

ROW 20: (RS) With MC, k7, [k1, p1] 3 times, k8.

Work Rows 1–8 once more. BO all sts in patt.

Block as described on page 33.

FRONT

With two strands of CC held tog and straight needles, CO 81 (93, 105) sts. Cut yarn. With WS facing, join MC. Rep Rows 1 and 2 of Relief chart until piece measures 4 (4¾, 5½)" (10 [12, 14] cm) from CO, ending with WS Row 1 of patt. With two strands of CC held tog, work Rows 18 and 19 as for gauge swatch.

NEXT ROW: (RS) K7, *[k1, p1] 3 times, k6; rep from * to last 2 sts, k2.

Rep Rows 1–16 of Relief chart until piece measures 14¼ (15¾, 17¼)" (36 [40, 44] cm) from CO, ending with a WS row.

Shape Neck

Keeping in patt, work 35 (41, 47) sts, join new yarn and work 11 sts then place these 11 sts on a holder for front neck, work to end of row—35 (41, 47) sts rem each side. Working each side separately, at each neck edge, BO 3 sts 1 (2, 2) time(s), then BO 2 sts 2 (1, 2) time(s), then BO 1 st (2, 3, 3) times—26 (30, 34) sts rem each side. Place sts on holders for shoulders.

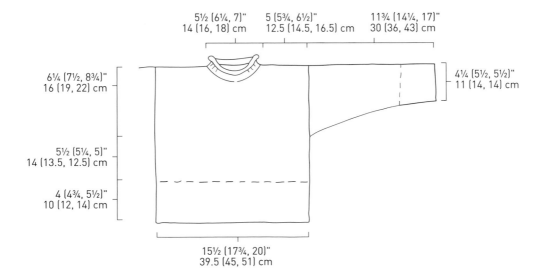

5½ (6¼, 7)" 14 (16, 18) cm

5 (5¾, 6½)" 12.5 (14.5, 16.5) cm

11¾ (14¼, 17)" 30 (36, 43) cm

6¼ (7½, 8¾)" 16 (19, 22) cm

4¼ (5½, 5½)" 11 (14, 14) cm

5½ (5¼, 5)" 14 (13.5, 12.5) cm

4 (4¾, 5½)" 10 (12, 14) cm

15½ (17¾, 20)" 39.5 (45, 51) cm

Relief

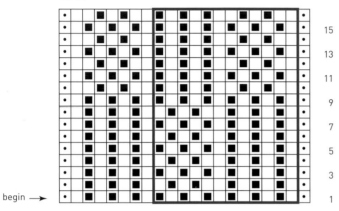

begin →

15
13
11
9
7
5
3
1

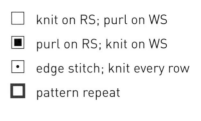

☐ knit on RS; purl on WS

■ purl on RS; knit on WS

· edge stitch; knit every row

☐ pattern repeat

BACK

CO and work as for front until piece measures same as front to shoulders, eliminating neck shaping. Place sts on holder.

JOIN FRONT AND BACK AT SHOULDERS

Place 26 (30, 34) held right front shoulder sts on one needle and 26 (30, 34) corresponding right back shoulder sts on another needle. Hold the pieces with RS facing tog and use the three-needle method (see Glossary) to BO the sts tog. Rep for other shoulder—29 (33, 37) sts rem for back neck.

SLEEVES

Measure down and mark 6¼ (7½, 8¾)" (16 [19, 22] cm) from shoulder on front and back. With one strand each of MC1, MC2, and MC3 held tog, straight needles, and RS facing, pick up and knit 69 (81, 93) sts evenly spaced inside the edge sts between markers. Work Rows 1–5 of chart.

DEC ROW: (RS; Row 6 of chart) K1, ssk, work in patt to last 3 sts, k2tog, k1—2 sts dec'd.

Work Rows 7–16, then rep Rows 1–16 and *at the same time* dec 1 st each end of needle as for dec row every 4th row 11 (11, 17) more times—45 (57, 57) sts rem. Work even if necessary until sleeve measures 9¼ (9¼, 11½)" (23.5 [23.5, 29] cm) from pick-up row, ending with WS Row 1. With two strands of CC held tog, work Rows 18 and 19 as for gauge swatch.

NEXT ROW: (RS) K7, *[k1, p1] 3 times, k6; rep from * to last 2 sts, k2.

Rep Rows 1 and 2 of chart until piece measures 11¾ (14¼, 17)" (30 [36, 43] cm) from pick-up row, or desired total length. BO all sts.

FINISHING

Weave in loose ends. With MC threaded on a tapestry needle, use the mattress st (see Glossary) to sew side and sleeve seams. Block to measurements.

Neckband

With one strand each of MC1, MC2, and MC3 held tog, cir needle, RS facing, and beg at left front shoulder seam, pick up and knit 19 (21, 23) sts along right front neck to held front sts, work across 11 held sts, pick up and knit 19 (21, 23) sts along left front neck to held back sts, work across 29 (33, 37) back sts—78 (86, 94) sts total. Work in k1, p1 rib for 1¼" (3 cm). Change to two strands of CC and knit 6 rnds. BO all sts, allowing edging to roll.

abbreviations

beg(s)	begin(s); beginning	rep	repeat(s); repeating
BO	bind off	rev St st	reverse stockinette stitch
CC	contrasting color	rnd(s)	round(s)
cm	centimeter(s)	RS	right side
cn	cable needle	sl	slip
CO	cast on	sl st	slip st (slip 1 stitch purlwise unless otherwise indicated)
cont	continue(s); continuing		
dec(s)	decrease(s); decreasing	ssk	slip 2 stitches knitwise, one at a time, from the left needle to right needle, insert left needle tip through both front loops and knit together from this position (1 stitch decrease)
dpn	double-pointed needles		
foll	follow(s); following		
g	gram(s)		
inc(s)	increase(s); increasing	st(s)	stitch(es)
k	knit	St st	stockinette stitch
k1f&b	knit into the front and back of same stitch	tbl	through back loop
		tog	together
kwise	knitwise, as if to knit	WS	wrong side
m	marker(s)	wyb	with yarn in back
MC	main color	wyf	with yarn in front
mm	millimeter(s)	yd	yard(s)
M1	make one (increase)	yo	yarnover
p	purl	*	repeat starting point
p1f&b	purl into front and back of same stitch	( )	alternate measurements and/or instructions
patt(s)	pattern(s)	[ ]	work instructions as a group a specified number of times
pm	place marker		
psso	pass slipped stitch over		
pwise	purlwise, as if to purl		
rem	remain(s); remaining		

glossary

BIND-OFFS

Standard Bind-Off

Knit the first stitch, *knit the next stitch (two stitches on right needle), insert the left needle tip into the first stitch on the right needle (Figure 1) and lift this stitch up and over the second stitch (Figure 2) and off the needle (Figure 3). Repeat from * until one stitch remains on the right needle. Cut yarn and pull tail through last stitch.

Three-Needle Bind-Off

Place stitches to be joined onto two separate needles. Hold the needles so that right sides of the knitting face together. Insert a third needle into the first stitch on each of the other two needles (Figure 1) and knit them together as one stitch (Figure 2), *knit the next stitch on each needle the same way, then use the left needle tip to lift the first stitch over the second and off the needle (Figure 3). Repeat from * until no stitches remain on first two needles. Cut yarn and pull tail through last stitch.

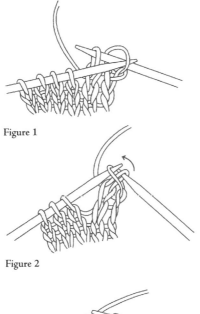

Figure 1

Figure 2

Figure 3

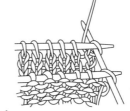

Figure 1

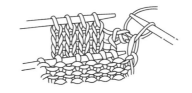

Figure 2

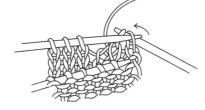

Figure 3

CAST-ONS

Backward-Loop Cast-On

*Make a loop in the working yarn and place in the needle backwards so that it doesn't unwind. Repeat from *.

Knitted Cast-On

Place a slipknot on the left needle if there are no established stitches. *With the right needle, knit into the first stitch (or slipknot) on the left needle (Figure 1) and place the new stitch onto the left needle, twisting it as you do so (Figure 2). Repeat from *, always knitting into the last stitch made.

Figure 1

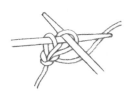

Figure 2

Long-Tail (Continental) Cast-On

Leaving a long tail (about ½" to 1" [1.3 to 2.5 cm] for each stitch to be cast on), make a slipknot and place it on the right needle. Place the thumb and index finger of your left hand between the yarn ends so that the working yarn is around your index finger and the tail end is around your thumb. Secure the ends with your other fingers and hold your palm upward, making a V of yarn (Figure 1). Bring the needle up through the loop on your thumb (Figure 2), grab the first strand around your index finger, then go back down through the loop on your thumb (Figure 3). Drop the loop off your thumb and, placing your thumb back in the V configuration, tighten the resulting stitch on the needle (Figure 4).

Figure 1

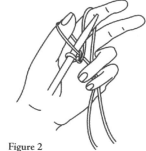

Figure 2

Figure 3

Figure 4

DECREASES

Knit Two Together Through Back Loops (k2togtbl)

Knit two stitches together through the loops on the back of the needle.

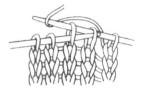

Purl Two Together Through Back Loops (p2togtbl)

Bring right needle tip behind the first two stitches on the left needle, enter through the back loop of the second stitch, then the first stitch, then purl the two stitches together.

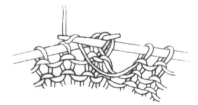

Slip, Slip, Knit (ssk)

Slip two stitches individually knitwise onto right needle (Figure 1). Insert the point of the left needle into the fronts of the two slipped stitches and use the right needle to knit them together through their back loops (Figure 2)—one stitch decreased.

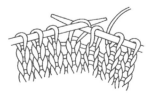
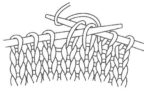

 Figure 1

 Figure 2

Slip, Slip, Slip, Knit (sssk)

Slip three stitches individually knitwise (Figure 1), insert left needle tip into the front of these three slipped stitches, and use the right needle to knit them together through their back loops (Figure 2).

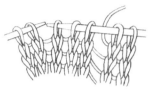
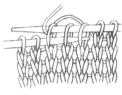

Figure 1   Figure 2

EMBROIDERY

Buttonhole Stitch

Working into the edge half-stitch of the knitted piece, *bring tip of threaded needle in and out of a knitted stitch, place working yarn under needle tip, then bring threaded needle through the stitch and tighten. Repeat from *, always bringing threaded needle on top of working yarn.

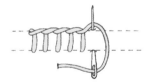

Duplicate Stitch

Bring threaded needle out from back to front at the base of the V of the knitted stitch you want to cover. *Working right to left, pass needle in and out under the stitch in the row above it and back into the base of the same stitch. Bring needle back out at the base of the V of the next stitch to the left. Repeat from * for desired number of stitches.

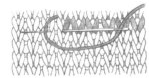

INCREASES

Knit One Front and Back (K1f&b)

Knit into a stitch and leave that stitch on the left needle (Figure 1), then knit through the back loop of the same stitch (Figure 2) and slip the original stitch off the needle (Figure 3)—one stitch increased.

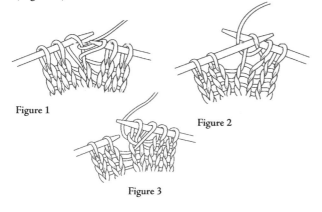

Figure 1

Figure 2

Figure 3

Make-One (M1)

With left needle tip, lift the horizontal strand between the stitches on the two needles, going from front to back (Figure 1). Knit the lifted strand through the back loop to twist the strand (Figure 2)—one stitch increased.

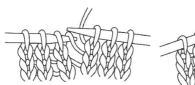

Figure 1

Figure 2

Make-One Purlwise (M1 pwise)

With left needle tip, lift the strand between the needles from back to front (Figure 1), then purl the lifted loop through the front (Figure 2).

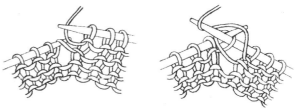

Figure 1

Figure 2

PICK UP AND KNIT STITCHES

Along Bind-Off or Cast-On Edge

With right side facing and working from right to left, *insert needle tip into the center of the stitch below the bind-off or cast-on edge (Figure 1), wrap the yarn around the needle, and pull a loop through to the front (Figure 2). Repeat from *.

Figure 1

Figure 2

Along a Shaped Edge

With right side facing and working from right to left, *insert needle tip between two stitches, warp the yarn around the needle, and pull a loop through to the front. Repeat from *, picking up about three stitches for every four rows, unless otherwise instructed.

POM-POM

Cut two circles of cardboard, each ½" (1.3 cm) larger than desired finished pom-pom width. Cut a small circle out of the center and a small wedge out of the side of each circle (Figure 1). Tie a strand of yarn between the circles, hold circles together and wrap with yarn—the more wraps, the thicker the pom-pom. Cut between the circles and knot the tie strand tightly (Figure 2). Place pom-pom between two smaller cardboard circles held together with a needle and trim the edges (Figure 3). This technique comes from *Nicky Epstein's Knitted Embellishments*, Interweave, 1999.

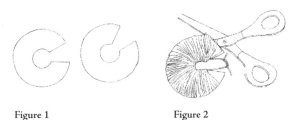

Figure 1   Figure 2

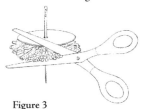

Figure 3

SEAMS

Mattress Stitch

Place the pieces to be seamed on a table, right sides facing up. Begin at the lower edge and work upward as follows for your stitch pattern:

Stockinette Stitch with One-Stitch Seam Allowance

With right side of knitting facing, use threaded needle to pick up one bar between the first two stitches on one piece to be seamed (Figure 1), then pick up the corresponding bar plus the bar above on the other piece (Figure 2). *Pick up the next two bars on the first piece, then the next two bars on the other (Figure 3). Repeat from * to the end of the seam, finishing by picking up the last bar (or pair of bars) at the top of the first piece.

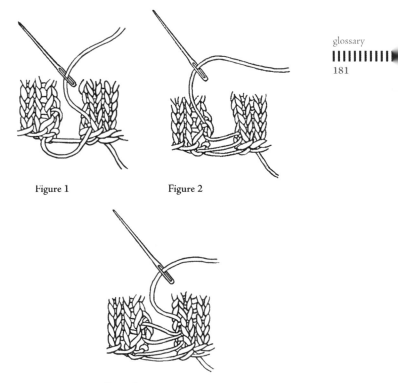

Figure 1   Figure 2

Figure 3

Stockinette Stitch with One-Half-Stitch Seam Allowance

To reduce bulk in the mattress stitch seam, work as for the one-stitch seam allowance but pick up the bars in the center of the edge stitches instead of between the last two stitches.

Garter Stitch

Insert threaded needle under the lower purl bar between the two edge stitches on one piece, then the upper purl bar from the stitch next to the edge stitch on the same row of the other piece.

Reverse Stockinette Stitch

With the right sides of the knitting facing you, use the threaded needle to *pick up the lower purl bar between the last two stitches on one piece, then the upper purl bar of the edge stitch on the other piece. Repeat from *, always working in the lower purl bars on the first side and the upper bars on the other (otherwise, the purl bars will be mismatched at the seam).

TASSEL

Cut a piece of cardboard 4" (10 cm) wide by the desired length of the tassel plus 1" (2.5 cm). Wrap the yarn to the desired thickness around cardboard. Cut a short length of yarn and tie it tightly around one end of the wrapped yarn (Figure 1). Cut yarn loops at the other end. Cut another piece of yarn and wrap it tightly around the loops a short distance below the top knot to form the tassel neck. Knot securely, thread ends onto a tapestry needle, and pull to the center of the tassel (Figure 2). Trim ends.

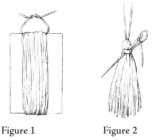

Figure 1   Figure 2

ZIPPER

With right side facing and zipper closed, pin zipper to the knitted pieces so edges cover the zipper teeth. With contrasting thread and right side facing, baste zipper in place close to teeth (Figure 1). Turn work over and with matching sewing thread and needle, stitch outer edges of zipper to wrong side of knitting (Figure 2), being careful to follow a single column of stitches in the knitting to keep zipper straight. Turn work back to right side facing, and with matching sewing thread, sew knitted fabric close to teeth (Figure 3). Remove basting.

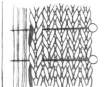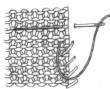

Figure 1   Figure 2   Figure 3

index

sources for yarn

All of the yarns used in this book are by Marianne Isager and are distributed in the United States by:

Tutto Santa Fe
137 W. Water St.
Santa Fe, NM 87501
(505) 989-9930
tuttosantafe.com

Laceweight (#0 Lace)
Alpaca 1 (100% alpaca; 875 yards [800 meters]/100 grams)
Wool 1 (100% wool; 667 yards [610 meters]/100 grams)

Fingering Weight (#1 Super Fine)
Alpaca 2 (50% merino, 50% alpaca; 558 yards [510 meters]/100 grams)
Bomuld (100% cotton; 459 yards [420 meters]/100 grams)
Bomulin (75% cotton, 25% linen; 459 yards [420 meters]/100 grams)
Highland (100% wool; 547 yards [500 meters]/100 grams)
Viscolin (50% viscose, 50% linen; 405 yards [370 meters]/100 grams)

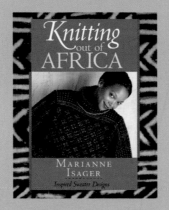